on track ...
Nektar

every album, every song

Scott Meze

sonicbondpublishing.com

Sonicbond Publishing Limited
www.sonicbondpublishing.co.uk
Email: info@sonicbondpublishing.co.uk

First Published in the United Kingdom 2023
First Published in the United States 2023

British Library Cataloguing in Publication Data:
A Catalogue record for this book is available from the British Library

Copyright Scott Meze 2023

ISBN 978-1-78952-257-0

Typeset in ITC Garamond & ITC Avant Garde
Printed and bound in England

Graphic design and typesetting: Full Moon Media

on track ...
Nektar

every album, every song

Scott Meze

Would you like to write for Sonicbond Publishing?
We are mainly a music publisher, but we also occasionally publish in other genres including film and television. At Sonicbond Publishing we are always on the look-out for authors, particularly for our two main series, On Track and Decades.

Mixing fact with in depth analysis, the On Track series examines the entire recorded work of a particular musical artist or group. All genres are considered from easy listening and jazz to 60s soul to 90s pop, via rock and metal.

The Decades series singles out a particular decade in an artist or group's history and focuses on that decade in more detail than may be allowed in the On Track series.

While professional writing experience would, of course, be an advantage, the most important qualification is to have real enthusiasm and knowledge of your subject. First-time authors are welcomed, but the ability to write well in English is essential.

Sonicbond Publishing has distribution throughout Europe and North America, and all our books are also published in E-book form. Authors will be paid a royalty based on sales of their book.
Further details about our books are available from www.sonicbondpublishing.com. To contact us, complete the contact form there or email info@sonicbondpublishing.co.uk

Follow us on social media:
Twitter: https://twitter.com/SonicbondP
Instagram: https://www.instagram.com/sonicbondpublishing_/
Facebook: https://www.facebook.com/SonicbondPublishing/

Linktree QR code:

on track ...
Nektar

Contents

Introduction

Exiled geographically and spiritually from prog rock's heartland, Nektar have struggled to gain not just the seat at the high table they deserve but presence in the room. A band that sold extremely well, that was one of the very few British acts to crack America, and that made two of prog's pinnacle albums during the genre's golden age can't even warrant a mention in most books on the subject. Even though Nektar are the epitome of what prog is supposed to represent – including widescreen, multi-textured structures, side-length suites, narrative concept albums, instrumental dexterity, even lyrical depth – they somehow don't fit the template. This book is an attempt not just to celebrate one of Britain's most underrated bands but to set the record straight.

The deeper you dive into Nektar, the more singular a band you uncover, and the more of those uneasy prog conventions you realise they bucked or transcended, which may go some way to understanding their ostracism.

For example, Nektar doesn't fit into the cliché of prog as the music of an upper class or intellectual elite. None of its members used an ability in classical music as their hook, like Keith Emerson or Rick Wakeman. They didn't claim roots in a prestigious university town or develop art school pretensions – both of which apply to the band they most resemble, Pink Floyd. They didn't even have the good grace to come from the south. In fact, their origins in the country's industrial centres of Sheffield, Coventry, and Rotherham place them closer to their two major and acknowledged influences – The Beatles and The Moody Blues – both of which grew fruitful music from barren soil.

Nor did they lord it over the rabble beneath, to use one of the music industry's gripes against prog. Nektar weren't funded by a rich patron and they didn't make much money of their own. The uncomfortable truth about the band, like so many in the genre that we now revere, is that they were all but penniless throughout the golden age.

British they may be, but the fact that Nektar soon abandoned their home country to seek greater reward in continental Europe is also a strike against them for a genre that always found it hard to accommodate artists from outside the home counties. This places them in the same boat as Frank Zappa, say, a man who toured with and admired the band. Zappa's every musical breath ought to place him at the very heart of the genre. He was earlier, more radical, more establishment, and more transgressive than almost all his British equivalents, but he also struggles to gain space in its texts.

I use 'texts' here pointedly. Prog's fans, among whom I proudly count myself, have the most liberal taste of any musical genre. We don't just fill our heads with reggae or rap or jazz or folk to the exclusion of all other styles. We listen to and assimilate everything from Opeth to Pauline Oliveros. We'll switch at a beat from wailing guitars to wailing Bulgarian throat singers. We relish Nektar among all the other flavours in our collections. It's the rock journalism that grew up in the same golden age that is the problem. Even as prog burgeoned in Britain, its weekly music papers became squalid, self-centred, and cruelly opinionated. It was the press that sidelined bands like Nektar, and so rehabilitating the band means building on the void where their media foundations ought to be.

Most notably, the British music papers never knew where to place the band. Since they were based in West Germany, they must be part of the West German scene, which was characterised as freaky and primitive: shag-haired Neanderthals clanging trance rhythms and blooping rudimentary electronics to accompany blockhead mushroom trips. It hardly mattered that the derogatory label 'krautrock' applied only to a small subset of German bands. Nektar, by the dismissive pigeonholing of the age, must be one of them.

Typical of this view was Ian MacDonald, whose three-part overview 'Krautrock: Germany Calling' in *New Musical Express* in December 1972 derided the country's 'prevailing anti-cerebral climate' and the 'generally rather bovine contemplations' of bands such as Tangerine Dream. MacDonald called upon a fellow *NME* journalist, Tony Stewart, to stick the ultimate early-1970s dagger in: 'If there were any British bands five years out of date, they'd go down a storm in Germany at the moment.'

In reality, Nektar were the most visible of a rich seam of melodicists on the continent. The correct category is not alongside Ash Ra Tempel and Guru Guru but with bands such as Eloy, Grobschnitt, Novalis, and Triumvirat, France's Atoll and Gong, Finland's Wigwam, or even the symphonic bands from Italy. They never forsook hummable tunes, relatable lyrics, and soulful singing. They rewarded listeners with the perfect blend of tightness and extemporisation. Their solos soared without a glimpse of showboating. And their fluidity of sound was less constipated than so many of their British rivals, more daringly open to the flow of the moment, and far warmer in its effect than just about anybody I can think of, save perhaps the more smiling of the Canterbury bands.

Besides, the cross-pollination of British and West German bands was richer and more ingrained than MacDonald's musical snobbery allowed. The country had been, after all, the staging post for much of the beat boom, had a network of US military bases hungry for Anglo rock'n'roll, tuned greedily into radio stations broadcasting to those troops, and had flowered into the world's third-largest market. Nektar were only one British band, along with others such as Message and Light Of Darkness, that went there to hone their craft and stayed, finding themselves among a host of West German bands with British members, including Twenty Sixty Six And Then, Abacus, Amon Düül II, Between, Blackwater Park, Epitaph, and Slapp Happy. Then there were UFO, a British band who gained success when they added German guitarist Michael Schenker, and British bands such as Bachdenkel and Sindelfingen that gave themselves German-sounding names.

Moreover, West Germany was open-eared. It was every bit as musically daring and inventive in the early 1970s as Britain and had a far stronger claim to its radicalism. Here was home to Karlheinz Stockhausen, a towering classical composer with impeccable avant-garde credentials who, almost uniquely among the grand old men of his time (he was 42 in 1970), thoroughly embraced psychedelia. Like Can and many others, Nektar visited Stockhausen, listened to Stockhausen, and revered Stockhausen. There was simply nothing remotely similar to inspire young performers in Britain.

Here too were drugs in wild profusion – a landscape of hallucinogens far deeper and less paranoid than Britain's – and vast stoned audiences that wanted to be transported. Here was a hippie culture that hadn't been beaten into the dust as it had in Britain and the US, and a youth that had legitimate, achingly evident grounds for rejecting everything its parents' generation stood for. Here was an infrastructure of outrageously talented producers such as Dieter Dierks in well-equipped studios to cater, without interference, to every crazy fantasy the bands could devise, and labels that, perhaps in sheer incomprehension, were willing to release the results.

It's no wonder that the British prog bands all gravitated to West Germany. Many found a ready audience there, as did artists such as David Bowie in their wake. Or that West German electronics, inspired by Pink Floyd's pioneering work with sequencers, became the dominant voice in all of pop.

But if the British press refused to understand you – there were also, naturally, historical reasons for the weeklies to hate West German music – then you weren't in the press, and if you weren't in the press, then you'd lost the bulk of your visibility. Why should listeners seek you out? The least we can say is that Britain in the early 1970s was awash with musical talent. If kids didn't know you, they had plenty of other options to latch onto.

Nektar did themselves no favours by making little attempt to play in the UK for years. But could there have been a living there for a band of their style? They could have slaved, as Hawkwind did, to gain notoriety as a druggy space rock act. They could have struggled on the alternative and free festival scene – to have played Glastonbury Fayre in 1971, for instance, shoving their van through muddy fields to flapping, tarpaulin-covered stages like Mighty Baby or Kingdom Come – but like them, they would surely have remained an also-ran.

West Germany was, in fact, the perfect incubator for a wayward band like Nektar. In his 1996 memoir *Rhinos, Winos & Lunatics*, Deke Leonard explained exactly what made the country so attractive to Man, a band who were musically very similar to Nektar in their early years:

We had totally given up on Britain. The occasional gig we did there was poorly attended and never covered by the press. Our gig circuit was comprised entirely of Cook's Ferry Inn, where our average audience was about 15 in number. In Schorndorf, it was 2,000.

Never covered by the press: hence the dismal numbers. Man spent six months in West Germany, living as guests in Nektar's communal home, and considered staying there permanently. Those six months certainly honed the band's drug-baked meanderings, making them one of the most enthralling of the age. They achieved their British breakthrough only when they managed to befriend a *Melody Maker* journalist, Roy Hollingworth, who became their proselytizer. On such tiny events do empires rest. Nektar had nobody shouting for them in the weeklies and had to build their British following the hard way: through word of mouth and blind curiosity, by kids stumbling on albums in import shops like Richard Branson's and wondering just what the grooves sounded like in a thing so intriguing and strange.

Ironically, while Man never managed to heave themselves out of the pub rock scenes in which they found their British audiences, Nektar – with really no commercial motive for the advance – bootstrapped themselves up to a pair of grand symphonic rock albums, *Remember the Future* (1973) and *Recycled* (1975), which place them at the upper flight of the genre. Almost despite themselves, they were a huge hit in the US, a country to which they immediately and disastrously relocated.

How, then, was this feat accomplished? Whatever prog rock fans like me might want to suppose, it was so rarely due to the brilliance of the albums themselves. For all that prog turned its nose up at singles, mainstream radio play was the surest way to success. A hit could take even a band as contrary as Hawkwind into the stratosphere.

At the very least, your work needed something that FM programmers could broadcast. Bluntly, and heavily reductively, Yes were a huge success because they found themselves on American radio. Van der Graaf Generator were not because they didn't. With 'Roundabout' a calling card, albums as crazy as *Close to the Edge* (1972) and *Tales from Topographic Oceans* (1973) could sell in bulk even if they weren't easily boiled down to broadcast material. Genesis, for all the column-inch wildness of Peter Gabriel's stage antics, sold very little before the 'I Know What I Like' single (1973) gave radio a handle to crank. They became a phenomenon only when they began to concentrate on the format.

Even Pink Floyd, which had floundered for years, suddenly began selling by the juggernaut when American radio latched onto 'Money' as something rocky and intriguing it could spin. *The Dark Side of the Moon* (1973) soared in the charts *before* the track was extracted as a single.

Nektar's brief bloom in the US was due to FM radio programming jangly, commercial extracts from *Remember the Future*. The band's tenure there was short, not least because they tried, like Genesis, to shift to singles but never produced anything remotely resembling a hit. The commercial failure of their pop-questing *Magic is a Child* LP in 1977 shut the door firmly on the band's hopes. Punk and new wave were irrelevant to their fortunes. Supertramp, another similar British band that ought to have been ditchwater dull by 1979, instead became superstars on the back of the hit-laden *Breakfast in America*. Nektar simply didn't get the break.

9

But here's yet more of the injustice meted out to Nektar. Practically from the start, they folded commercial rock into their mix, the antithesis of prog's image of itself in those years before *Dark Side* prompted everyone to do it. There *should* have been hits. Perhaps the band's own impatience was the issue, their unwillingness to buff their best songs into international sonic sweetmeats. Hits rely so often on their trickery. For their third album *...Sounds Like This* (1973), Nektar bashed out a whole double LP's worth of fine material live and raw, largely in order to be rid of the songs so that they could concentrate on developing new material – a little more care could have made *that* the breakthrough. Instead, its unpolished edges mean the album is one of the band's least regarded from the period.

Ultimately, the looseness and agility of the early band played against them. Whereas Pink Floyd's peak albums were hewn painstakingly from an unyielding band rockface – torturous writing and recording sessions over many months, grinding against the band's own inertia and lack of inspiration – Nektar had energy and creativity to spare. They couldn't wait to see what they could come up with next. And with yet more irony, whereas Floyd connoisseurs like myself rate highly the album that slipped through the cracks, the soundtrack LP *Obscured by Clouds* (1972) that the band threw together in a couple of weeks largely, I suspect, for a working holiday in France, Nektar's golden age is a whole career full of *Clouds* which seem to be damned for being so unassuming. You get the feeling that if the US hadn't happened, Nektar could have careened onward after *Recycled* to all kinds of marvellous new diversions.

Still, there's absolutely no mystery why this struggling band, years into their provincial poverty, leaped on the US. We'd all have done the same. It was simply unfortunate that they couldn't maintain momentum there. Just as had happened in the UK, they received no love from the American music papers. The band managed just one half-page article in *Rolling Stone*, in November 1974, which concerned itself most with their jury-rigged, underpowered lightshow, and just one brief album review, a savage beating of *Remember the Future* by Paul Gambaccini the following month:

> The pretentious lyrics are hardly decipherable. Lead singer Roye Albrighton is thankfully able to keep a straight face while singing about a bluebird who blesses a blind boy with wisdom and sight – although his voice does become strident at times.

Great as it was, *Recycled* was not the smash that turned the band into a global phenomenon. Nektar themselves blamed poor distribution by their US label. Subsequently, tensions tore the band apart, and the golden age was over at the very moment it should have begun to pay dividends.

Afterwards, Nektar spluttered, lay dormant for two decades, spluttered again, and released the bulk of their material – simply in terms of playing time – in albums that both strained to recapture the youthful abandon of the golden age and yearned to move beyond it to remain relevant to an ever-changing audience. In this, at least, Nektar are more closely aligned to the other old-school prog bands that have rejuvenated themselves in the past two decades. They are both a heritage act and an act that needs to attract younger fans. They dazzle, they connect, they play beautifully and they fill the room, but they are only partly a rock band. They are also partly a theme park. There is no prog survivor in the current and very welcome resurgence of the scene, save perhaps King Crimson, that doesn't struggle with this dichotomy.

Many of us equate our fandom to the lengths by which we are willing to follow a band. Do we move onward through the downturn? I hesitate to characterise those attracted to Nektar, but I would expect that most listeners are either primarily or wholly interested in the golden age. For all Nektar fans, the gateway drug is surely the six studio LPs up to *Recycled*.

I get that. As the writer of a band overview, it means I must do what prog writers so often do, which is to concentrate mostly on the 1970s. I don't need to convince you who already revere the later band to jump on board. You're way ahead of me, leaping around in delight every time Nektar roll into your town or release a new disc. But for those less familiar with the band, here's a comprehensive guide to what you need: the core albums that are going to impress you the way they impress me, and the means by which you can move your fandom forward to a host of newer works that are unfairly overlooked like so much else of this hidden treasure of a band.

Enter K: Nektar's identity and anonymity

Stop someone in the street and ask them to name a member of classic era Yes or Genesis and they could probably dredge up one or two candidates. An even sketchily educated prog fan could likely trot out the lead figures in King Crimson, Jethro Tull, and Van der Graaf Generator. They'd give you a blank stare regarding Nektar.

Even more than Pink Floyd, the prog rock act that traded most on their facelessness, Nektar replaced the personality of their players with the immersive, anonymity-inducing power of their lightshow. For both bands, the lights and effects were compensation for a fairly static stage presence. Alternatively, they liberated the players to concentrate on their music. You didn't need to jump about if the lights provided all the movement and excitement for you. For the audience, it made the players all but irrelevant. You got off your head on drugs and the event provided what nightclubs have provided ever since: a barrage of beats and strobes to divorce mundane mind from ecstatic daze.

In this, of course, both bands were following a pattern laid down in 1966 by lightshow pioneers in the US, in particular the psychedelic maelstrom at the Fillmore Auditorium in San Francisco. Lightshows were a boom business in the late 1960s. No event or underground club was complete without one, and a host of providers vied for the business with ever brighter, more enveloping lights, trippier effects, and more sophisticated syncopation and empathy with the sounds.

Mick Brockett was typical of this. His Fantasia Light Circus provided 'definitely the best lightshow in Europe' (according to its business card) to Pink Floyd and others in 1968. The following year he crossed paths with a band called Prophecy, which invited him to join them permanently when they renamed themselves Nektar in January 1970. Brockett would not only operate the lights. He would be a fifth member of the band, with a fifth share of their income. As their following erupted across West Germany, at least in part on the back of Brockett's spectacle, he hired an assistant, Keith Walters. Both men are pictured on the inside gatefold of Nektar's first album *Journey to the Centre of the Eye* (1971), as integral members of the band. Walters quit in 1972, but Brockett remained with the band throughout the golden age and indeed returned to the group for their most recent renaissance in 2019.

The others, though – well, who cared about them? For what it's worth, Prophecy comprised guitarist/vocalist Colin Edwards, organist Allan Freeman, bassist Derek Moore, and drummer Ron Howden. In 1968 they were a typical British beat band paying their dues, as beat bands had done since before the days of The Beatles, playing cover versions of soul and pop hits in the dive bars of Hamburg's Reeperbahn. While Prophecy were resident in the Star-Club, another British beat band called Rainbows were over at the Top Ten. With nothing else to do during the day, Rainbows guitarist Roye Albrighton took to hanging around the Star-Club and jamming with Howden. They hit it off, so when Edwards quit a year later, Albrighton was first on Prophecy's list.

Did Prophecy acquire a singer and guitarist, or did Albrighton acquire a backing band? The answer depends on whether you subscribe to the cult of celebrity, and it was this that Nektar seemed determined to avoid. For sure, he's the first among equals, the closest Nektar had to a lead presence, and the man who merely by dint of singing most of the songs is most associated with their lyrics, even though, in common with Peter Gabriel, Ozzy Osborne, and Geddy Lee, he wasn't necessarily the man who wrote them.

The blurring of their members into Nektar anonymity was accentuated by the band's decision to run as a true democracy. Just like the Doors, Deep Purple, Black Sabbath, and others, they understood that their music was a group effort and hence merely listed the band as composer. Regardless of who instigated the melody or words, everybody added *something* to the mix. Like Genesis's 'all titles done by all' note on the back of *Selling England by the Pound* (1973), so all Nektar's music up to *Recycled* is credited merely to 'Nektar.'

For sticklers of accuracy, this causes a headache. For all those albums, I want to list the four musicians alphabetically: Albrighton, Freeman, Howden, Moore. However, the 2011 compilation *Retrospektive 1969–1980* is the first release to try to disentangle that 'Nektar' credit and it adopts the listing Albrighton, Howden, Freeman, Moore – a slightly non-alphabetical order that I nevertheless adhere to religiously in this book. The BMI database concurs that these four men are the writers of the songs, whatever their order. And yet it's likely not true. The band claimed, with justification, that even though Brockett didn't sing or play an instrument, he was part of the creative process. The band developed much of their material by improvising live onstage. Brockett's lights inspired and guided those improvisations, and hence contributed to the music. He ought also to get a credit.

In 2004, Albrighton explained the band's writing process to *Progressive Ears*:

The way we used to do it in the old days was someone would come up with the idea. Ninety per cent of the time, it was the guitarist, although it could be Taff [Freeman] on the keyboards. So we'd come up with something and everybody would work on it and we'd take it out on the road with us, sort of half-finished, and we'd slop it into the middle of the existing set and segue through that from one song to another, and see what people's reactions were. That way, we'd be able to not only rehearse it, but each night we'd add a bit more to it until it ended up being a 15- or 20-minute piece of music. At which time we would then take it out again, strip it apart, add some more pieces to it, and before you know it we'd have an album and then we'd give some kind of storyline to it.

Howden told *Sound & Vision* in 2020:

> The chemistry [between the four musicians] was unbelievable. We would just be playing together, and suddenly a whole album would come out of it. It was like: 'What? We've just been playing the music we like to play, and you're telling me that's an album?'

Moore, however, has noted that he and Brockett would write lyrics together. Whether this means all of them is unclear since surely Albrighton had some input. He'd been writing his own songs since the days of Rainbows. But again, it suggests an injustice in following the *Retrospektive*/BMI convention in omitting Brockett. Indeed, the ...*Sounds Like Swiss* set (2021) credits everything to Albrighton, Howden, Freeman, Moore, Brockett in that order, perhaps an oversight righted now that Brockett was back in the team.

Conversely, Albrighton told *Sea of Tranquility* in 2011:

> Yes, [Brockett] was portrayed as a fifth member but only in the live arena. Essentially, he left the musical compositions and performances to us and we left the lights to him.

At first, the band had no idea whether Albrighton would mesh well with the others. They knew two things: that this new Prophecy would phase out playing cover versions and write all their own material, and that they wanted to dive into the burgeoning prog waters by playing bluesy, psychedelic jams inspired by Vanilla Fudge. So in November 1969, they staged a low-key gig at the German youth club in which they rehearsed simply to test the chemistry. As Moore told *Progressive Rock Journal* in 2021:

> We decided if it went down badly, we would tell the reporters we were called Pollen, and if it went down well, it would be Nectar.

Presumably coincidentally, a band named Pollen *did* form in Canada in 1972, releasing one very well-received symphonic LP in 1976. More curiously still, the French band Pulsar, whose sound is very similar to Nektar, released an album called *Pollen* in 1975.

The experiment worked. Nectar it was – but with a puzzling change of letter. And here's the thing. If you live in Germany and you want to be thought of as a German band, give yourself a German name. If you don't, then it's probably not the best idea. European prog is full of bands whose native K gives an otherwise familiar word a distinct regional flavour: Alkaloid, Arktis, Cyklus, Ikarus, Kluster, Kollektiv, Kraftwerk, Oktober, and Spektakel in Germany, Aktuala in Italy, Ekseption in the Netherlands, Anekdoten and Kornet in Sweden, Krokodil in Switzerland, and many more. Nektar seems to fit in among these for the wrong reason. There's only one other British band of the style that comes to mind from the golden age: Cirkus, named from the 1970 King Crimson track, which was meant to make a circus sound unfamiliar and frightening, just as lyricist Pete Sinfield would repeat later with ELP's 'Karn Evil 9'.

Why, then, the K? In the *Retrospektive 1969–1980* booklet, Albrighton claimed band innocence:

> We thought we would be different by spelling it with a K, but never realised that that was the German way to spell nectar.

Moore suggested to *Velvet Thunder* in 2000 that the K was added 'to make it sound a bit more like a hard rock band.' Nektar's goal was to toughen up the wishy-washy C. But surely they understood that the Teutonic rock label had a heritage, first exploited by the cover of Led Zeppelin's second album in 1969 and the same one that later prompted Blue Öyster Cult and Motörhead to adopt their umlauts? If the latter's association wasn't clear, then Lemmy's Nazi biker image left no doubt, and it's an affectation that heavy metal bands have imitated ever since: we pummel like a blitzkrieg. That's why the US tech metal band named themselves Vektor. To this day, the Stahlhelm-evoking spelling has never seemed to fit with Nektar's more nuanced, less bludgeoning style of rock. See the name in isolation and you'd likely think the band weightier than they are and file them next to Scorpions.

Meanwhile, individual anonymity was further deepened when the band decided on a group logo in 1971. The 'beeman' – a sort of insectoid patchwork anatomical diagram with a skeleton guitar – first made its appearance on second LP *A Tab in the Ocean* (1972) and has become the band's registered trademark, a continuity through all their changes alongside cover paintings by their designer Helmet Wenske. In truth, it's a repugnant, clumsy, over-fussy logo (we're very far removed from Roger Dean's Yes symbol) that no teenage fan is going to scratch on their school desk. Band awareness isn't much aided by the unreadable NEKTAR word treatment that sits alongside it. Still, there are worse prog emblems – go ask Gentle Giant. And the band's name did gift Nektar a strand of bee imagery that has enabled them to look attractive when they want.

The anonymity of the covers is not itself a differentiator. One of the ways in which rock separated itself from pop was by refusing to place its band members on the front cover of new studio releases. Even a band as attractive and with such mainstream potential as The Moody Blues had pushed for that change as far back as 1967. Live albums excepted, a very few long-running British bands of the golden age never once appeared on their front cover: Budgie, Camel, Genesis, Jade Warrior, and a handful more. (Alas, Hawkwind broke their admirable run on *Road to Utopia* in 2018.) Most appeared rarely. Nektar have shown their faces a grand total of once, pointedly, mostly dressed as clowns, on the cover of *Down to Earth* (1974).

The four performers and Brockett formed one of prog's most stable units. Throughout the golden age, nobody joined, nobody left. But in the wake of the failure of *Recycled* in 1976, Albrighton quit, subsequent to which the band embarked on a whirligig of short-term members and guest players. Albrighton's replacement Dave Nelson (not the man from New Riders Of The Purple Sage), lasted just one album before Albrighton returned. This line-up soon tore itself apart again, resulting in a 1980–82 phase of the band which saw Albrighton as the sole remaining original member.

After their long hiatus, Albrighton and Freeman pieced the band back together in 2000, bringing the original Nektar onto the stage again at NEARfest in 2002, for which Brockett provided the lights. But this, too, didn't last, with Moore quitting quickly and Freeman leaving for good in 2003.

Albrighton and Howden led a series of line-ups until the former's death in July 2016. We then witnessed one of rock's periodical eye-rolling occasions in which two incarnations vied for the same name and audience. The remnants of Albrighton's band, led by long-term keyboard player Klaus Henatsch, continued as (New) Nektar, while Howden, Moore, and Brockett put together a competing group. The least we can say is that this would not have been possible were the band not quite so anonymous: that personalities should matter more than brand name, even in an age in which established prog bands continue to tour simply by having one or two old-time members alongside their irrelevant others.

There's no love lost between the two incarnations, with Moore strongly claiming his band's legitimacy not just through their original members but by aligning themselves with Albrighton. *The Other Side* (2020) even works in an unreleased 1974 track, 'The Devil's Door', to boost its credentials.

My own feelings on which version represents the 'true' Nektar are complex and conflicted since they cut to the quick of notions of heritage and progression, as I explain in the introduction to *The Other Side*. Knowing full well any decision I make is bound to piss off *somebody*, I omit New Nektar's *Megalomania* (2018) from this book. Each reader will need to decide for themselves whether that was the correct call.

In search of sight: blindness and vision in the lyrics of Nektar

Though bees and the beeman are the recurring visual imagery in Nektar's albums, their primary lyrical imagery concerns sight.

Perhaps this is only to be expected of a band whose extra dimension was a lightshow. The audience is invited to come and see further, deeper, and both inside themselves and outward to the cosmos. All these voyages – literally evoked in the title *Journey to the Centre of the Eye* – are there in the hallucinatory effects of Brockett's slides and lens-work.

Moore told *Rolling Stone* in that solitary half-page article in 1974:

We're going for a total concept where people are even more involved...a feeling that you're inside something rather than looking at something.

And Freeman elaborated to Jeff Burger the same year:

Generally, what we want to do is take the audience away completely. Surround them with sounds, visuals, a total theatrical environment. When they leave the concert, we want them to have had an experience they'll never forget. We want to have reached them in as many ways as possible.

A stoned or tripping audience, too, would surely associate the giant startled eye on the cover of *Journey* with David Bowman's 'ultimate trip' at the end of the 1968 movie *2001: A Space Odyssey*, which repeatedly cuts from Bowman's experiences to his own dazed and dilated eye. A second giant eye adorns the inside gatefold of the *Sunday Night at London Roundhouse* LP (1974), subtly equating that circular venue with another communal awakening eye, while eyes and circle motifs reoccur from *...Sounds Like This* and *Remember the Future* all the way to the deluxe edition of *A Spoonful of Time* (2012).

My suspicion is that a great deal of this was inspired by The Moody Blues, whose own quest for pure vision formed a recurring theme in their albums. 'You've got to make the journey out and in,' as Mike Pinder sings on *To Our Children's Children's Children* (1969), an album that equates the Apollo program with mankind's searching for higher consciousness. On the cover of *Every Good Boy Deserves Favour* (1971), an old man, perhaps blind, offers a small boy a glowing treasure: illumination passed as simply as LSD.

Journey was, of course, the overture to a career, the primal text on which all the others would elaborate. Albrighton described its message to *It's Psychedelic Baby* in 2012 as 'using your mind's eye to look inside yourself to see the real person within'. To *Something Else!* in 2012, he noted of the concept's genesis:

The theme of outer space intrigued us but we wanted a different take on it, so we thought about inner space and seeing the world through different eyes.

Lyrically, the damaged psyche is cast as the obstructed eye from the start – 'my mind is gently weeping' – but when the mind's eye is opened, it is too much for the astronaut to bear. 'Now the sense that stops me going blind makes me wish that I was drinking wine,' he says in 'Burn Out My Eyes'. If mental oblivion isn't enough solace, there's the ultimate answer: 'destruction of the sense and the burning of my eyes.'

But even this isn't the end of the vision. The astronaut passes onward through the pupil of 'the all-seeing eye', God's fixed gaze scrutinising the universe. With his merging into this divine view, he is finally redeemed. He returns sobered by the enormity of his vision: his home planet is on a course for destruction and there's nothing he can do to stop it.

This theme – the Earth heading for ecological collapse under our own hands – is another repeating motif in The Moody Blues' music (it's the concept of the 1970 album *A Question of Balance*) and one that Nektar also used repeatedly, beginning with their own album on the subject, *Recycled*.

The acid trip of 'A Tab in the Ocean' is also suffused in sight. 'Desolation Valley' opens with the exhortation to 'take a look around yourself and see what I see.' Blindness, it suggests, is the ultimate result of 'persecuted eyes', and a lack of sight remains the subject of 'Cryin' in the Dark' and 'King Of Twilight', as their titles suggest.

...*Sounds Like This* kicks off with 'Good Day', a song about the night of *Tab* finally passing away: 'I looked into the morning. What did I see?' It's a wonderful inversion into joy, the lifting of all the dark shadows of the previous two discs. 'New Day Dawning' acknowledges that night will return, but this is simply a natural cycle and it will pass in its turn. We next pick up the theme on 'Cast Your Fate', essentially a summary of everything we've learnt to date. 'I believe in all that's good,' Albrighton sings, 'like the blind man says I should.' The blind man is back in 'A Day in the Life of a Preacher', moving slowly and surely through life.

For its second grand narrative, *Remember the Future*, Nektar's blind man became a blind boy, but enlightenment came again from the stars through the agency of a telepathic alien that guides him to the truth. Bluebird has questions of his own – 'whose are the eyes of the world we're looking through?' – but his effect is wholly positive. The boy's exclamation 'I can see you!' is the most cathartic moment in the band's entire career.

Down to Earth might be a different kind of concept altogether, but it finds new ways to frame the same theme. In 'Astral Man', for example, there's 'close your eyes. Watch him fly.' 'That's Life' is a movement from darkness to illumination: 'He can see the nightmares, now he sees the light.' And 'Show Me the Way' is the plea for enlightenment that its title suggests. It even directly evokes Brockett's lightshow: 'Pictures all around, painted on the ground.'

Recycled repeats the story. Our coming doom is a darkness – we're 'nearing the end of the day' – but we can avoid it if we simply 'look'. Albrighton repeatedly urges us to open our eyes, but it is the choir at the end of part one that casts the theme in its finest, most triumphal despair: 'Do you see? Do you see?' The yearning is still there in the band's finest song, 'It's All Over'. 'See the daytime, you've seen the darkness,' Albrighton sings. 'I'm torn apart through those many changes.' It's supposed to make you cry to close the circle back with *Journey*, and it does. No other band save The Moody Blues so neatly sewed up their run of classics.

Afterwards, Nektar's sight imagery is less prevalent but still recurs in surprising places. 'Magic is a Child' is about a child 'opening my eyes in the morning'. 'Listen', the one song on *Magic is a Child* co-written by Albrighton, concerns a singer 'blinded by veils we hang to avoid the truth'. On 'Angel' from *Man in the Moon* (1980), Albrighton mourns that 'I'm not seeing you'. 'Do you see it now like I do?' he asks on 'Far Away'. On 'Can't Stop You Now', he notes that 'this world is more to the eye than understanding'. The theme's most direct in 'You're Alone': 'as your darkness sets in, don't be blind.'

By *The Prodigal Son* (2001) – whose cover image oddly refracts that of *Every Good Boy Deserves Favour* – Albrighton has himself taken on the guise of the weary old man rather than the bright-eyed boy. 'It's so hard for me to see how you all stand and bleed,' he sings on 'Now'. On 'I Can't Help You' he tells us: 'I've spoken to guardians of light, time that you think with your eyes.' 'Camouflage to White' kicks off *Evolution* (2004) with: 'when reality finds you, the days of your life open up before your own eyes.' 'Child Of Mine' is a tender invitation to a baby to 'open your eyes.' And 'Phazed by the Storm,' the awakening of Albrighton's spirituality after a near-death event, praises God in turns of trippy enlightenment: 'you gave me more than just a vision.'

But as Albrighton aged, new shadows took over from the heavenly light of the band's grand quest. 'Where Are You Now' in *Book of Days* (2008) expresses regret for a vision that has slipped away, directly invoking *Remember the Future*: 'bluebird remember me.' Albrighton's final album *Time Machine* (2013) struggles to move forward on 'A Better Way': 'just look into my eyes, the answer to all your dreams.' There's the feeling that it wasn't, and that there is defeat in the final closing of his eyes.

Unsurprisingly, when Moore and Brockett wanted to reconnect with their past on *The Other Side*, it was also *Remember* that was invoked: 'I see your eyes to see the world' on 'Skywriter', something beyond the darkness of life in the instrumental 'The Light Beyond', and like a summary of everything that has gone before in 'Look Thru Me', perhaps as much a final tribute to Albrighton as to the band's merging of light with sound, 'a painting finally finds its wall.'

Journey to the Centre of the Eye (1971)

Personnel:
Roye Albrighton: guitar, lead vocals
Allan 'Taff' Freeman: keyboards, vocals
Ron Howden: drums
Derek 'Mo' Moore: bass, Mellotron, vocals
Recorded: June to August 1971 at Dierks Studios, Stommeln, West Germany
Producers: Dieter Dierks, Peter Hauke, Nektar
Released: Bacillus Records LP, November 1971 (West Germany)
Running time: 42:01 (A: 20:47 B: 21:14)

The band's heads were in a very good place by the time it came to record
this debut album. Not only had the experiment to integrate Albrighton into
Prophecy's sonic world proved a resounding success, but the team was soon
pooling new ideas and writing music of ever-increasing complexity and
engagement.

Having settled in a communal house in the village of Seeheim, close
to a psychedelic club in Darmstadt called The Underground that offered
Nektar a residency and a manager, there was no longer the worry that West
Germany wouldn't accept the band. Audiences grew steadily larger and more
enthusiastic, eventually resulting in a huge and dedicated fanbase. Albrighton
told *Progressive Ears* in 2004:

> We'd built a reputation as a unique live band because we always tried to do
> something new. Most other bands [in West Germany] at the time were just
> playing Beatles songs, Rolling Stones, a bit of soul. We tried a few ideas and
> it became very popular and we found ourselves being asked back again and
> again, and a following grew, to the point where between '74 and '76 we
> were playing major theatres. First in Germany, then it spread out to Holland,
> then France, Switzerland, and the rest of mainland Europe.

Moore agreed in a 2020 interview with *Velvet Thunder*:

> We were definitely less influenced by the mainstream in the UK. The
> German scene was very different. They didn't want to hear pop music. They
> were hungry for anything new, so we played none of the pop stuff. We still
> had outside influences: The Beatles, Vanilla Fudge, The Moody Blues, and
> the Man band, who were around with us too, but certainly, we were trying
> to keep to ourselves as much as possible so that we could produce our own
> music.

Songs never took over completely from jams, but as the band built their
repertoire, the long, meandering excursions became integrated into definitive
structures, in the same way as had worked so well for Pink Floyd and The

Grateful Dead, whilst they also became a means to introduce and develop new material, which was not true of those antecedents. Jamming for hours and then plucking out ideas to develop was a style of writing that places Nektar more in the company of bands like Can, which were based 100 miles away in Cologne.

Moreover, as Moore had noted to *Velvet Thunder,* the musicians soon had kindred spirits Man to inspire them. Albrighton noted in the *Retrospektive 1969–1980* booklet: 'I think a little of their music rubbed off on us, and a little of ours on them.' Indeed, *something* revolutionised the Welsh band in the gap between the fussy, self-transfixed *2 Ozs of Plastic with a Hole in the Middle* released in September 1969 and their looser and more confident follow-up, the untitled LP recorded in October 1970 that blurred strong songs with driving jams and culminated in 'Alchemist', a 20-minute collapse into coma. That something was surely West Germany in general and Nektar in particular.

Drugs were undoubtedly part of the advance. If Prophecy's and Rainbows' experiences were typical, their work on the Reeperbahn was fuelled mostly by the chemicals of endurance, just like The Beatles and all the others. Down in Darmstadt, the drugs of choice were hallucinogens – and in vast abundance. Deke Leonard chronicled the culture shock of moving from London's furtive joint-cupping scene to The Underground's pronoiac abandon in *Rhinos, Winos & Lunatics*:

> The club was a long, dark, arch-roofed cellar. There was a wall, two feet high and a foot wide, running along the front of the stage. As we set the gear up, I noticed a lump of something lying on the top of the wall. It was an eighth of an ounce of soapy, black dope. As gig-time approached, the air got heavier and heavier with the beautiful smell of marijuana. By the time we walked onstage, there wasn't a molecule of oxygen left in the place. During the set, a procession of people walked up to the stage and nodding their appreciation, placed a piece of dope on the wall. By the end of the gig, the wall was piled high with all kinds of dangerous drugs.

In an interview with *Prog* in 2020, Moore chuckled at the memory: 'It was an awesome scene.'

Communal living also seemed to work for Nektar the way it did for many other West German bands. The Seeheim house – that's the kitchen in the *Journey* gatefold – offered a rehearsal space that facilitated creativity, surely including input from Man during the six months their members were living there. By the summer of 1970, a long narrative piece had begun to coalesce and soon began to edge out the band's other material in live performance, aided by Brockett's thematic lightshow. This 'space opera' (to use the band's own term) progressed as far as 'Warp Oversight' before the band ran into a creative block, completing the sequence first with renditions of 'Good Day' and 'New Day Dawning' before settling on the ignominious splashdown of what would become 'Desolation Valley'. This at least gives structure to 'Waves', the astronaut awaiting rescue in his floating capsule and resigned to his failure. However, eventually, all the band's water imagery was shelved for their equally conceptual second album *A Tab in the Ocean* and a means was found to keep their adventurer out in space.

Where did the piece come from? Musically, to the expected rock band influences must be added Stockhausen, whom the band encountered in Darmstadt. Albrighton, Howden, and Deke Leonard have all noted Stockhausen's influence on Nektar at this time. His more radical vision was intertwined with the band's patchwork of sources – songs, jams, motifs, ideas – plus sound effects and the inspiration of Brockett's lights. Albrighton told *Something Else!* in 2012:

> It all sounded a little trippy and, if you like, spacey. So we decided to sit down and devise a story encompassing the sounds we had created, and a theme that had never been used before.

Well, to a degree. What's curious about *Journey* is not that it was a narrative piece about a trip through space – that's as old as Offenbach's 1875 opera *Le Voyage Dans La Lune*, Holst's 1917 suite *The Planets*, or for that matter, Joe Meek's *I Hear a New World* (1960) or Attilio Mineo's *Man in Space with Sounds* (1962) – but that there were at least four close antecedents that were also space-related, and all four also happened to be debut albums.

There's nothing new, revolutionary, or even notable about a 1970s 'concept' album. All albums are conceptual because all albums package together music based on a collective theme or style or artist. It's practically signalled by the name 'album', a curated package of discs that were presumably not pulled together at random. (If they *were* that itself might be called a concept.) Lyrical themes as we know them began with Frank Sinatra in the 1940s. By the 1950s, even Elvis Presley was releasing thematic albums. How pretentious of him.

Narrative concept albums, those that tell a story from start to finish, likely began with cast productions of Broadway shows, movie soundtracks, and renditions of large-scale classical works, opera, tone poems, and narrated sequences such as Prokofiev's 1936 work *Peter and the Wolf*. The earliest *rock* narrative, as far as I can tell, is *The Psychedelic Sounds of the 13th Floor Elevators*, released in October 1966. It purported (though not very convincingly) to chronicle the quest for higher consciousness through LSD. The first rock album to tell a comprehensible tale was British band Nirvana's debut album *The Story of Simon Simopath* the following year, which, for lack of anything better to call it, the band labelled 'a science fiction pantomime.'

So here's the first of our close antecedents. In *Simon Simopath*, the titular protagonist is an astronaut on his first space mission. In Earth orbit, he encounters an alien who begs him for food. Simon's reward is a fabulous ride to a paradise planet. The exact same story was reinterpreted as a parable about the circles of time for the second side of The Small Faces' *Ogdens' Nut Gone Flake* in 1968. That year, Dutch band Group 1850 released the second close antecedent, *Agemo's Trip to Mother Earth*. Here, it is the paradise-dwelling alien that comes to Earth only to find it a hellscape of cruelty and violence. The only hope for mankind is the hippies, so he guides them back to his home.

The third and fourth, both released in 1970, showed the concept darkening even more. In *A Time Before This* by Julian's Treatment, Earth has already been destroyed by our own folly. A last man travels to Alpha Centauri, where he becomes embroiled in yet another conflict. In Magma's untitled first album, a group of human survivors make the exodus and build a new life for themselves on the planet Kobaïa, but apocalyptic war ensues.

How many of these antecedents Nektar were aware of is debatable. Perhaps none. Magma's album was not released until October 1970, by which point we can assume that much of *Journey* was in place. (Paul Kantner's *Blows Against the Empire* can also not have been an influence since it was not released until November.) But Nektar's story feels a little undeveloped compared to the others. Our world is at war. An astronaut encounters aliens in space and is taken to their home, where he learns the secrets of the universe and is returned, chastened and horrified, in time to witness the destruction of our squabbling sphere. There's no welcome intervention for the rest of us. No hope, in fact, at all, since our alternatives are either to be pulverised by nuclear bombs or maddened by the hard gaze of reality.

Moving forward, Daevid Allen would reimagine the story yet again for Gong's *Radio Gnome Invisible* trilogy starting in 1973. Allen, it seems to me, spent much longer reaching the same conclusion, whereas Magma never quite reached it at all.

However earnest the theme and striking the presentation, the prototype *Journey* found it difficult to attract a taker. Finally, Peter Hauke signed the band to his Bacillus Records label, soon to be folded into the vast Bellaphon empire. Hauke handed the group over to Dieter Dierks, owner of an 8-track studio built on the grounds of his parents' house in Stommeln on the far side of Cologne. He'd achieved success quickly, thanks to the excruciatingly catchy pop hit 'Loop Di Love' by Juan Bastós (about an encounter with a prostitute, no less), but is better known today as the bastion of the *kosmische* school of West German rock. Before Nektar rolled in, he'd already been involved in albums by Gila, Ihre Kinder, Hairy Chapter, Orange Peel, and Tangerine Dream. Among other benefits, Dierks's studio boasted a Mellotron, the same one that forms a strand through the German music of that time. It is, of course, employed on *Journey*. The first three Nektar albums were recorded there, and all the discs up to *Down to Earth* mixed in the facility.

Dierks recorded each of the two sides of *Journey* separately and in one pass since there was concern that the 8-track tape couldn't be spliced – the same concern that had led Pink Floyd to perform the whole of 'Atom Heart Mother' in one pass at Abbey Road the year before. He was heavily involved in the album's sound (he's supposed to have performed some uncredited piano on it), but essentially, Nektar produced themselves, an extraordinary claim for a band with almost no prior studio experience. Albrighton admitted to *It's Psychedelic Baby* in 2012:

> One of my strongest memories of this album was: can we get away with this? It was maybe a little too far out for some people, but hey, what the hell! We just went ahead and did what we wanted and threw caution to the wind.

There is, finally, some confusion as to whether *Journey* should be considered a narrative made up of 13 individual tracks or a single track with 13 sections. All releases, to my knowledge, have presented it as tracks – that's certainly the way it appears on the original banded Bacillus vinyl. If the latter were the case, it would have some cachet as a pioneer ahead of Jethro Tull's *Thick as a Brick*, recorded the month after it was released. But under its own criterion, it could not be the first single-track LP in rock. The same claim could be made for a host of albums from as far back as 1967 if you want to include Ceyleib People's *Tanyet* and The Moody Blues's *Days of Future Passed*, or 1968 if you don't: Zappa's *Lumpy Gravy* (released as 'Part I' and 'Part II'), Joan Baez's *Baptism* (presented as 'Part One' and 'Part Two'), Joni Mitchell's *Song to a Seagull* (presented as 'Part 1' and 'Part 2'), Van Morrison's *Astral Weeks* (the sides are labelled 'In The Beginning' and 'Afterwards'), and, most pertinently given its influence on the band, Vanilla Fudge's *The Beat Goes On*.

All songs composed by Albrighton, Howden, Freeman, and Moore.

'Prelude'

There were two strands of space music by the time Nektar began work on *Journey*: the poppy, outer space frolics inaugurated by the likes of 'Telstar' by The Tornados and 'Mr. Spaceman' by The Byrds, and the darker, more punishing – and likely more realistic – vision of space as lonely, disorientating, and depersonalising that filtered through from science fiction into Pink Floyd. The live disc of *Ummagumma* (1969) provides a full primer for space rock. It's cold, brutal, and its voyages are dark and dangerous trips. Pink Floyd is most certainly the touchpoint for Nektar since Hawkwind, the band who most fully developed the Floyd's ethos, did not release their manifesto second album, *In Search of Space,* until October 1971, a narrow month before the release of *Journey*. Other influences outside those I mentioned in the album introduction seem to me less likely. Sure, the band must have known David Bowie's 'A Space Oddity' (1969), but that rehash of *2001* adds nothing but attitude: space as a disconnected vacuum. Bowie's astronaut heads into orbit, has his mind blown by the beauty he sees below, and drifts off into druggy oblivion.

This brief instrumental opener reveals the Floyd influence clearly. It even begins like 'Astronomy Dominé' with a spooky throbbing beat against the zippy space particles of Albrighton's corkscrewing guitar slide. A plummeting scale on Moore's bass evokes 'Interstellar Overdrive' (from the 1967 album *The Piper at the Gates of Dawn*), while Freeman's majestic church-style organ chords bring to mind the 'Storm Signal' section of 'A Saucerful of Secrets'. The only question so far is whether Nektar are going to be more than the mere sum of their influence.

'Astronaut's Nightmare'

A descending staircase riff shifts us into what will become the standard Nektar sound: aching minor key verses that resolve into huge soulful refrains, though the band hasn't yet developed their trademark soft funk beat. Instead, the section is all frantic early prog, driven by Freeman's strident Hammond and punctuated by insane scribbles of Albrighton's electric guitar. The latter's swirls of low slide and channel-hopping, bubbly sounds give the piece a distinctly psychedelic flavour, again akin to early Pink Floyd, which – just like the Floyd – the band will gradually expunge from their sound over the next two years.

Conceptually, the sleeve note gives us the first episode in the album's plot. This is apparently somewhat in our future since the first thing we hear is a computerised voice (the equivalent of Bowie's ground control) identifying itself as 'Robot 13' – Earth is teetering on the edge of nuclear war. Nevertheless, a one-man rocket is headed off to Saturn of all places, purpose unknown. Lyrically, our unnamed astronaut is not having a good time, even at the start of his odyssey. He knows that Earth is about to die, and therefore everything he loves will soon be gone, let alone that he won't have anywhere to return to. Isolated out there in the void, he broadcasts his own tinny radio transmission into the dark, pleading for God to help him.

Here, too, is the first instance of the band's own ambiguous grammar, one that will form just as rich a strand into the future. The original Bacillus cover omits the apostrophe in the title, though it has been added often enough since for me to include it here.

'Countenance'

The next three pieces are all instrumental, which is awkward since they have a lot of narrative to express. In this section, we learn from the liner notes that the astronaut's prayer is answered by an alien 'saucer' which intercepts his vessel and takes him on board. The aliens tell him that they've been 'observing Earth for many years' but are 'surprised at our warlike ways' – surely those two statements are mutually exclusive? Regardless, they offer the astronaut a tour of their 'galaxy' and off they go.

Since this must involve fabulous technology, you'd think they might bother to intervene – but no. Like UFOs since time immemorial, it's okay to interact with lone individuals, but the prime directive keeps them hidden, I suppose.

Musically, all this must be imparted to anyone who doesn't have the LP sleeve to hand by a drifting minor-key riff, similar to the slower part of 'Astronaut's Nightmare', on a haunted bed of Mellotron that picks up into a thundering guitar solo and searing chords triumphal in their despair.

'The Nine Lifeless Daughters of the Sun'

This section shoves us abruptly into a jazzy prog workout for Hammond and guitar over Moore's up-and-down bass runs, already with glimpses of his chunky mature sound, and Howden's mechanical beat. It gathers, again, to a blasting band workout. The idea is to suggest a vast Krell-like machine shoving the saucer at phenomenal speed across the universe.

Like 'Countenance,' the meaning of the title is obscure. It may be intended merely to add extra mental associations to drug-enhanced aural voyages. (See the first side of *Recycled* for more of these.)

'Warp Oversight'

'Daughters' culminates with a sonic meltdown into this sequence of disconnected rhythmless sounds, annihilating blips, Richard Wright-style organ chop, guitar squalls, and bass bluster, all bathed in a vast cosmic reverb designed to expand your mind into the furthest reaches of space. It's effective, too: an eternity floating among the fleet passages of stars and rocks and the occasional gloopy suck of black holes. Conceptually, it's a description of the saucer's journey through hyperspace and its eventual arrival at the aliens' home galaxy.

'The Dream Nebula (Part 1)'

Let the astronomers quibble that there's a fundamental difference between a galaxy and a nebula. Anyway, here we are in a galaxy that is 'so serene and beautiful' that it causes the astronaut to experience 'incredible dreams'. These are expressed by grand ringing chords meant to blow off the lid of your skull.

The title is slightly ambiguous. The original back cover simply calls it 'The Dream Nebula' and its repeat over the LP flip as 'The Dream Nebula Part II'. More ambiguity regards the track or tracks themselves. 'Part 1' runs 2:16 and 'Part 2' 2:25. There's an overlap of slightly more than a minute in which the band plays a short song section – the first vocals we've had in a long time – to end side one and then reprises it, verbatim, on a gradual fade-in to begin side two. Clearly, given the issue with the 8-track tape, this was not simply the same piece of music spliced twice into the master but was performed as a repeat. Fair enough: other albums that express a single piece of music over two sides do the same, rather than simply fade out and in, including Magma's *Mekanïk Destruktïẁ Kommandöh* (1973) and Yatha Sidhra's *A Meditation Mass* (1974). To my knowledge, no stereo CD version has omitted the overlap, though the 5.1 layer of the 2004 SACD does. What's more perplexing is that in live performance, the band routinely performed the section *twice* as if it isn't actually an overlap at all, simply the same piece played two times in a row.

'The Dream Nebula (Part 2)'
Having repeated the song to open the second side of the LP, the rest of this section continues the drift with Albrighton's flecks of golden guitar over the band's most majestic chord changes.

'It's All in the Mind'
For the first half of this piece, Freeman steps forward to sing a simple ballad about how our astronaut has seen too much beauty and feels overwhelmed by it all. The accompaniment is a throwback to 1960s Mellotron pop, heavy on both the strings and flute tapes. You can imagine this fitting in perfectly on a Moody Blues album. The second half leans on insistent bass triplets to explore a short stretch of high-octane prog rock, including some squelchy electronics, before resolving back into the 'Dream Nebula' chords.

'Burn Out My Eyes'
Regardless of the no-splicing policy, the jolt here certainly does seem like an edit. We move after the briefest of silences to solo flute-tape Mellotron and acoustic guitar (with a strong nod to Pink Floyd's 1968 B-side 'Julia Dream') that gradually coalesce into the album's longest section by far (at 8:42), an agonising slow blues in which the astronaut's floundering mentality is expressed first by Albrighton's impassioned vocal alone through the disconnect of studio filtering, and then by full Moody Blues harmonies. Momentum is maintained, however, through asides into different musical textures, including a manic fast sequence with screaming twin guitars and harsh, Van der Graaf Generator-style organ abuse.

'Void of Vision'
The rhythm picks up again for yet another helter-skelter journey in which the astronaut whirls across 'a long, beautiful valley' (presumably on a planet of some kind) before being confronted with what, in shouty capitals, the liner note describes as 'a great shining EYE suspended in space – THE "ALL SEEING EYE"!' This horrible revelation, which may have been inspired by Philip K. Dick's paranoid 1957 novel *Eye in the Sky* – the eye here is, just like in the novel, an image of a cruelly staring God – is declaimed by Moore to discordant pop made to sound like lunatic players clinging to their instruments in a vortex of mental turmoil.

'Pupil of the Eye'

A little calm is afforded by more of the band's Moodies harmonies before the sequence kicks up the madness still further. This section skitters remorselessly forward with great belches of Hammond as Freeman and Moore describe in turn
the astronaut's capture and absorption by the giant EYE. Having achieved union with God, our hero is suddenly struck by the knowledge that this paradise world is actually our own planet if only we would stop bickering among each other.

'Look Inside Yourself'

The craziness resolves suddenly into this plea for our world to come to its senses, set against more flute Mellotron, but the madness soon returns.

'Death of the Mind'

We switch, finally, back to the 'Astronaut's Nightmare' tune for one final repeat of the opening refrain. We appear to be back where we started, with the astronaut moving through dark empty space toward Saturn and weeping for the folly of our species.

Though the album's sermon is simple enough, the narrative leaves this ending ambiguous. Did the astronaut *dream* all this? Was there never an alien encounter, never a trip through hyperspace, never the paradise Earth-without-war? And if it *did* happen, is he actually back in his ship now, or has he gone insane in the Dream Nebula? We learn only that 'his mind drifts back to his departure' which could mean either of these things, and that 'he visualises the destruction of Earth!' which doesn't *specifically* mean that the planet is destroyed, except the album closing so suddenly on its dramatic chords immediately after seems to suggest it does.

The point of the ambiguity, you might argue, is also obvious: the choice is ours. Which denouement do we want, global destruction or paradise planet? But the psychedelic experience is rarely so equivocal, and the trip of *Journey* is almost certain to come to an ugly end. I think it was this very problem, the risk of turning poor innocent trippers away from the message by giving them such a bad experience they won't touch the album twice, which prompted Daevid Allen to lighten his own version with humour. You need to balance your lows, as Allen understood, with twice as many highs.

Alternate versions and bonus tracks

The 2004 SACD release on Dream Nebula Recordings includes the entire album remixed into 5.1. I'm not sure of the providence of this mix. It sounds like an upmix from quadraphonic like the other multichannel releases (see the Collecting Nektar chapter at the end of this book for more), but to my knowledge, *Journey* was not released in quad back in the day. Perhaps quad was planned but not implemented. For this multichannel version, but not the stereo layer, the overlap part of 'The Dream Nebula' has been edited out so that the album runs seamlessly. Also included on this CD are both sides of the 'Do You Believe in Magic?'/'1-2-3-4' single that Bacillus pressured Nektar into recording. Reluctant or not, on its release in February 1972, the single was a hit in West Germany, greatly raising the band's profile there. Both sides were later rerecorded for *...Sounds Like This*.

'Do You Believe in Magic?'
Here's another of Nektar's fluid titles. The question mark comes and goes from release to release. This A-side (actually presented second on the CD) is a brightly unassuming piece of folk rock with a soaring chorus and lengthy scat-along guitar solo. It's not that significant by itself but it reminds me of the feel of other West German hippie anthems of the time, for example the single 'Too Many People' by Kin Ping Meh, released the previous year. Together they form an all but totally forgotten corner of the German rock scene of the period: anthemic ballads with melodies that yearn for acceptance in a busted world.

'1-2-3-4'
There are wars you choose to wage and those you are compelled to fight by circumstance. The former alone gives you a vehicle for protest songs, since few would argue the Allies should not have engaged with Hitler and let him butcher and exterminate his way across the world. Vietnam may well have been the band's target here, but there are inevitable layers of meaning in a song performed by a British band in post-war Germany playing for the children of that war's combatants. Reconstruction had not driven the old guard out of its government positions. There were still patriotic songs roared in bierkellers, still officers pulling the strings in West German society, still an undeniable contingent of kids who were growing up to be just like their folks.

Certainly, the youth that flocked to Nektar's concerts represented the anti-establishment end of the spectrum, those who abhorred Hitler's war and everything their parents had stood for, those willing to look on their own ugly history with the shame it deserved and signal their break from the past by long hair, communal living, drugs, and free love. For these, it was a complex act for their country's erstwhile enemy to lecture them on war – particularly one in which, even the most liberal child would concede, Germans had no choice but participate. But Nektar, perhaps, were more daring than the majority of Germans could be. The members were outsiders, after all. They could shove this uncomfortable mirror in the faces of their hosts, even if the only ones likely to hear the song's message were those who already agreed with its sentiments.

It's an ugly, strident piece which Albrighton screeches through a loudhailer like an officer cajoling his pawns to their slaughter. He even scats jauntily along to the guitar refrain, suggesting the bitter satire of Pink Floyd's 'Corporate Clegg' (1968) is being channelled here.

The 2013 CD release on Purple Pyramid includes a second disc containing a 46-minute live performance of the suite in Darmstadt on November 13, 1971. The 2016 CD release on Purple Pyramid includes both sides of the single and the entire Darmstadt gig on two extra discs. For more on this concert, see the Live Recordings chapter at the end of this book.

A Tab in the Ocean (1972)

Personnel:
Roye Albrighton: guitar, lead vocals
Allan 'Taff' Freeman: keyboards, vocals
Ron Howden: drums, vocals
Derek 'Mo' Moore: bass, vocals
Recorded: October 1972 at Dierks Studios, Stommeln, West Germany
Producers: Peter Hauke, Nektar
Released: Bacillus Records LP, November 1972 (West Germany)
Running time: 35:35 (A: 16:39 B: 18:56)

Having handled fire on their first album – the fire of passion, of suns, of
nuclear obliteration – Nektar moved on to water for their second. Air and
earth would follow. The obvious link between the first two is the water of the
eye, from 'weeping' on *Journey* to 'Cryin' in the Dark' here, but there are two
stated origin tales for the album. The first is that the band spent their days,
as you do when you're stoned from a wall's worth of gifted hallucinogens,
staring transfixed into their aquarium at home – those fish *know things*.
The second is that Walters had folded a wealth of nautical imagery into his
slideshow, and this too inspired contemplation.

When speaking to *It's Psychedelic Baby* in 2012, Albrighton was forthright
about these influences:

> Someone made a joke about what would happen if the oceans were spiked
> with LSD. After the laughter died down, we realized that we had a title for
> the new album, as the beginning was sounding a little oceanic in the riff and
> effects being used.

Despite managing only to consolidate their position in West Germany, the
UK still resisting them and the US a dream away, 1972 had been a very
good year for Nektar by the time they finally entered Dieter Dierks's studio
– now upgraded to a bigger, better room and 16-track tape – to record the
three pieces they had already been playing live for more than a year. This
most hermetical of bands was also networking of a fashion. The same year,
Freeman added Mellotron and vocals to fellow Bacillus signing Message's *The
Dawn Anew is Coming*. There would be very few other guest appearances of
this type.

Enthusiasm and creativity were higher than ever. There was no hassle, no
drama. Nektar knew what they wanted and achieved it with economy. And
at the end of the process, they still had energy to spare. Even while the band
was mixing *Tab* on 12 October, they were already laying down a first pass at
their next release, *...Sounds Like This*.

The immediate result was their most polished and beguiling early album.
The new confidence and poise were reflected in a more distinctive and

attractive sleeve than the debut. *A Tab in the Ocean* was the first Nektar album to be housed in a Helmet Wenske painting and the first to include the beeman logo. Its gatefold spread was far superior to the previous disc's dishevelled breakfast. Here, the six members (again including slides master Walters, his last album with the group) are posed in a psychedelic overlay of a wooden structure full of desert plants with burning gold highlights. Serious rock band conventions be damned: they're actually smiling.

The contents may seem less ambitious than *Journey*'s narrative concept, but actually, *Tab* feels like the more daring work due to it presenting an identical format to the same year's blockbuster *Close to the Edge*, released the month before the sessions started: one long statement on the first side, two weighty options on the second. Even the timings are similar. (Yes's album, in turn, may well have been influenced by Van der Graaf Generator's *Pawn Hearts* in 1971, which did the same except for flipping the sides.)

On paper, the eponymous 'Tab' track is the only side-filling piece by the band. In reality, Nektar produced two grand statements in this style, but the other – the first side of *Recycled* – is muddled in with the rest of that album by the questionable decision to split it into individual tracks and label it a 'Part One' – it's definitely not. *Recycled*, like *Tab*, consists of two halves: the side-filler and a second, associated side. Indeed, *Recycled* was never performed in its entirety, and only that side-filler became a live fixture.

'Tab', too, had a long and distinguished career as a live highlight. In fact, since the two suites on the second side were also performed regularly, *A Tab in the Ocean* has the distinction of being Nektar's most fully performed album. It may be largely overlooked by the prog cognoscenti, which never places 'Tab' among its masterworks, but the album is also one of the band's best. Perhaps the suspicion of gazing into space and its urbane technical modesty taint it for prog sticklers in the same way they do Pink Floyd's 1971 album *Meddle* – the loss is not ours.

All songs composed by Albrighton, Howden, Freeman, and Moore.

'A Tab in the Ocean'

Though it was soon castigated as prog's indulgence, it was actually psychedelia, not prog, that had made a habit of the 20-odd-minute, side-filling track. From Love's 'Revelation' in 1966 to whole-side suites and tracks by Hapshash And The Coloured Coat (*immensely* influential on West German rock), The Holy Modal Rounders, and The Mothers Of Invention in 1967, psychedelia was soon awash in the form. By 1968 they were commonplace, including the Amboy Dukes' 'Journey to the Center of the Mind' (from which surely some influence flowed), the Collectors' 'What Love', the hellfire side of The Crazy World Of Arthur Brown's sole album, Iron Butterfly's 'In-A-Gadda-Da-Vida', and The Steve Miller Band's 'Children of the Future'. Canned Heat's double LP *Living the Blues* even had the audacity to fill an entire *disc* with a single track.

With all this action, emergent prog had little actually to pioneer. By the release of *Tab* it was old news indeed. What had become important was not so much the length as the sonic adventure the track took the listener on, the various places it carried them. When Robert Wyatt (of resolutely long-form Soft Machine) noted that three-minute songs are boring, he was right. With a single, you usually know what you're getting within the first minute. The rest is predictable, a series of repeats. With a suite like 'Tab', you have no idea where you're headed, and that ability to go anywhere and do anything within the vast canvas of the 12-inch black disc is what made the form so enthralling.

Since in *Tab,* Nektar still bridged the two worlds of the psychedelic voyage and prog's more mannered, classically influenced structures, they still thought largely of their long piece as a means of evoking textures rather than an exercise in taxing the cerebellum. Prog would have no truck with their concept, the idea that enough LSD in the Earth's water supply would turn on everybody and everything. In the sober light of morning, the very thought is nightmarish, but at least the world was no longer blowing itself up with nukes. No, instead it was suffering something out of a Brian Aldiss or Angela Carter novel: a descent into unending foaming madness. So take Nektar's lyric largely as a joke. It's an invitation, Hendrix-style, to explore the drug-warped depths – there's even mention of Neptune. But 'Tab' offers no deeper meaning than this.

The music was designed to complement the sea-splatter blobs and oozing underwater life of Brockett's oil work. More prosaically, Walters would pull up slides of nautical imagery to guide those who lacked imaginations of their own, much the same way Pink Floyd would later use surfing footage from *Crystal Voyager* to accompany live performances of their own submarine epic 'Echoes'. But the trippy concept and accoutrements are misleading. The band had largely ditched the lysergic freeform of *Journey* in favour of tight, plotted sections of muscular prog rock, each musician working through an intricate ensemble piece which demanded they all lock together with the apparent telepathy that comes of long practice and live performance. It doesn't reward acid's mental maelstrom, and there are no trippy phasing, panning, and other effects.

Though the piece has a definite structure in that it begins and ends with the same symphonic theme, the rest is a series of restlessly shifting changes played one after another without pause, a musical grab-bag of ideas like glimpses of tracks the band was too impatient to develop. These, nevertheless, were played in sequence live, fragment A followed by fragment B followed by fragment C and so on all the way through the piece, with space to jam where appropriate or simply to move diligently through the patterns where not. In other words, it's as much program music as Gilmour-era versions of 'Interstellar Overdrive', which was also not at all psychedelic in its later years: each component played in order until the whole performance was completed.

33

Simply listing these changes gives no clue to their accumulative power, but here's what to expect. The track begins becalmed by organ drones and rolling electronic surf. At 0:39, Freeman's playing evolves into tumbling triplets over which Albrighton and Moore fuse in a weighty instrumental melody which I'll call the 'Theme'. At 2:21, this turns into a galloping section with chiming guitar chords. At 3:27, it relaxes to slower trance rock, over which Moore adds a half-recited statement of the pleasures of the ocean, his voice filtered to telephone thinness. This section becomes ever more strident until resolving on a restatement of the Theme at 5:00. There's then a pummelling riff with hard, military drumming at 5:37, embryonic Nektar funk with Albrighton's impassioned plea to dive in and find answers at 6:16, and a long punishing sequence of breakneck 6/8 rhythms from 8:05. This leads at 11:26 to brighter sections that sound like tryouts for the anthems of *Remember the Future*. At 14:16, it resolves back to Freeman's triplets and the final majestic restatement of the Theme. The piece blows itself apart on a power chord and a glimpse more of the surf.

'Desolation Valley'

The second side also consists of a single, unbroken piece of music, but it actually contains two suites cross-faded together, each a pair of tracks that were generally performed together. 'Desolation Valley/Waves' (5:43/2:29) grew out of early live versions of *Journey* in which the astronaut splashes back down to Earth after his encounter with the aliens, which of course, assumes that it hasn't been destroyed while he was floundering around near Saturn. Some versions shifted into what was originally called 'Acorn Valley' (and then became 'Porcelain Valley') directly after 'Warp Oversight', meaning that the hyperspace journey was not to the Dream Nebula but directly home.

It's a smoke-wreathed ballad with jazzy Hammond touches, a floating, ever-mutating bass line, and soft, understated guitar solos. Toward the end, it builds to a frenetic peak, like someone making one last attempt to drag themselves out of the water only to relax at once into the song's undulating riff, resigned forever to the sea's cold swell.

The lyric, as we have it on *Tab* and hence fossilised in live performance thereafter, is cryptic. The singer complains of 'persecuted eyes' and 'imagination merged with reality', both a clear kin to the *Journey* suite. The shift of title to 'desolation' mirrors the hero's state of mind throughout *Journey,* but also adds an all but suffocating bulk of other meanings due to the word's use in Bob Dylan's 1965 epic 'Desolation Row'. Dylan's nightmare housing unit was a ghetto of the mind populated by dropouts and failures. So, therefore, and inevitably, must be the Earth that the astronaut returns to. Any similar word – degradation, desecration, desperation, disillusion, dislocation, dissipation, and so on – would have expressed the same feeling without the Dylan associations, so we have to assume the link was intended.

'Waves'

A languid wash of cymbals, mallets, and cooing wordless voices eases us through this chilly stretch of empty water. Albrighton's exhausted spoken words wonder if anything is real.

'Cryin' in the Dark'

Weightless wah-wah guitars wreathe around each other, setting up a misleading expectation that this will be more of the melancholy of 'Desolation Valley/Waves'. Instead, 'Cryin' in the Dark/King of Twilight' (6:28/4:16) is a heavy rock workout that wouldn't sound out of place on an album by any of British rock's more mainstream metal bands of the period, though few of them would allow Moore his delicious excursions on bass.

The throwaway lyric here is merely a call for the singer's woman not to leave him in his moment of need, but the music has real power, with anguished anthemic guitar chords and a driving instrumental break over which Freeman, perversely, chooses only the laziest possible wanderings across his organ keys. Albrighton soon shoulders him aside to build a stinging mass of guitar noise like he's kicking over beehives right there on the stage. It all culminates in despairing soprano shrills in true metal diva style.

'King of Twilight'

Erupting breakneck out of this, 'King of Twilight' is more monstrous still, a bare-naked runaway horse ride through a desert of close-packed saguaro. Again there's not much in the way of a message, simply a call for freedom. The piece builds and builds, each part more thunderous than the last, before impaling itself abruptly on a very painful silence.

Alternate versions and bonus tracks

For its 1976 LP release in the US on Passport Records, the label requested that the album was remixed to beef up the sound. Moore and Larry Fast performed the remix, bringing up extra instruments on the multi-track, widening the stereo field, and artificially deepening bass frequencies. Both versions were included on the 2004 CD on Dream Nebula Recordings, and were released as a double LP by Purple Pyramid in 2013.

The 2011 CD release on ItsAboutMusic includes a second disc of the band's first studio recordings in Boston in 1970, here labelled *In the Beginning – The Boston Tapes*. For more on this session, see the Other Studio Recordings chapter at the end of this book. The 2013 CD release on Purple Pyramid includes both album mixes and a second disc of the entire album played live in Darmstadt on November 13, 1971. For more on this concert, see the Live Recordings chapter at the end of this book. It also includes the version of 'Desolation Valley/Waves' recorded for *The Old Grey Whistle Test* in 1973, though it fails to attribute the source. The footage is not included.

...Sounds Like This (1973)

Personnel:
Roye Albrighton: guitar, lead vocals
Allan 'Taff' Freeman: keyboards, vocals
Ron Howden: drums, vocals
Derek 'Mo' Moore: bass, vocals
Recorded: October 1972 ('Wings') and February 1973 (the rest) at Dierks Studios, Stommeln, West Germany
Producers: Peter Hauke, Nektar
Released: Bacillus Records LP, April 1973 (West Germany)
Running time: 1:14:24 (A: 17:15 B: 20:04 C: 18:46 D: 18:19)

It was crazy that a British band storming around West Germany for two years couldn't raise a whisper of interest in their country of origin. That was finally to change in June 1973, when Man's good word gained ...*Sounds Like This* a UK release on United Artists. In gratitude, Nektar name-checked the band on the cover of their next album, *Remember the Future*: 'Thanks to...the Man band (for coming to Germany).' At the time, UA also handled Hawkwind and Brinsley Schwarz, making it a shame indeed that Nektar couldn't have been around early enough to be invited to the Greasy Truckers Party at the Roundhouse in London in February 1972. Imagine how they would have filled out the resulting live album. Instead, Nektar blasted through the UK in support of *Sounds* and made their own triumphal appearance at the Roundhouse in November 1973. Europe's best-kept secret had finally arrived home.

UA was the perfect platform for the band. The label was already importing the cream of the West German scene into the UK, handling breakthrough albums by Amon Düül II and Can. It was also host to Cochise, Groundhogs, Help Yourself, and If, among many others – this was good company indeed. Nektar actually seem to be the anomaly in the roster, a band with a tighter, more constrained, more commercial understanding of what progressive rock signified. Hawkwind didn't begin to polish their sound until *Hall of the Mountain Grill* in 1974, perhaps seeded by Nektar's professionalism. None of the others lifted themselves to prog's top flight.

Regardless, UA might have thought it was getting yet another group of slack-limbed psychedelic rockers, given that *Sounds* was the band's least formal release to date – almost the entire double LP was laid down in just three sessions. Incidentally, the format itself was not an issue. Amon Düül II and Can had both released doubles on UA successfully, and Hawkwind put out *Space Ritual* that May to huge acclaim and sales. UA, moreover, had struck gold by printing Frank Zappa's *200 Motels* double set in 1971. As an introduction to a largely unknown band, it wasn't that daunting a package, but the album's discursiveness has counted against it ever since. We don't receive Nektar the same way we receive Hawkwind, say, a band revered for the skull-crushing spontaneity of their early discs but which lost much of their personality when they became a mainstream band, or Man, whose appeal is entirely with the slop and bluster of their improvisations. *...Sounds Like This* is damned for its heaviness, its unpolished immediacy, the idea that the band might actually be winging it. Prog's mouthpieces have even accused the album of having too much guitar.

Perhaps, actually, the set was merely mislabelled at the time and has been misunderstood ever since. The full title, *Nektar Sounds Like This,* signals the sonic equivalent of a business card, telling promoters and venue owners that they can book this baffling band with confidence. Exactly the same thinking lay behind the *Fortyfied* set 35 years later. In addition, the album's fairly simple design and that pedestrian title are both indicators of a back-to-basics approach – Nektar getting down to earth well ahead of time – that aligns the release with budget issues, such as those that enabled Richard Branson's Virgin label to introduce West German bands and Gong to Britain, even with the likes of the then-ubiquitous K-tel and MFP discs that you might pick up cheap in your local Woolworths. I'd rack it comfortably next to *Relics*.

Nektar certainly thought of it as a stop-gap album, one that they had begun during the *Tab* sessions and which merely cleared the deck in anticipation of *Remember the Future*. They recorded that epic a scant six months later. *Sounds* was meant as both introduction and closure, the belated appearance, in effect, of the first album they had attempted to record in Boston back in 1970. This doesn't mean you could slot it chronologically in front of *Journey* and feel gratified by the more regular progression in sophistication that results (and besides, *Down to Earth* will always be the stumble in *that* apparent stairway). It's an improbable double for the debut – not at all unprecedented since Zappa himself had done the same back in 1966, but unlikely – and its robust, confident sound is plainly the result of a band that had honed their craft and could play this material by muscle memory.

No, *Sounds* was a public gargle before the soprano sings. It has no right to be as good as it is.

Another double album gives us an extra perspective on the set. Pink Floyd's *Ummagumma* (1969) included a live disc partly in order that the band could catalogue away what they then considered elderly material so they didn't have to perform it anymore. Nektar, too, wanted to make space in their repertoire for the new pieces they ached to write. It would be neat to say that the difference is that the Floyd took years to write enough of the new material to effect the change – they were still performing three of the same four pieces at Pompeii in 1972 and again laid them down there to try to be rid of them – whereas Nektar soon had new material in plenty. Actually, some of the work on *Sounds* continued to fill out the band's live set for the rest of the golden age and beyond.

And claiming the album as a throwaway does it an injustice. True, Nektar first attempted to record it in an impromptu quasi-live performance in October 1972, perhaps because the *Tab* sessions had wrapped ahead of schedule and they still had the studio booked, but the band considered that tape inadequate and shelved everything they had recorded except for the four minutes of 'Wings'. They returned to the studio in February 1973 to try again, by which point some of the material had developed further. So there *was* a quality consideration, and Nektar *did* intend *Sounds* to reflect the band at their best in the circumstances, in front of an appreciative audience, that brought out their strengths. It's ironic that latter-day reviews of the CD with the earlier session as a bonus disc tend to focus on that material as its redeeming feature. An example is *Prog* magazine, which rubbished a reissue of *Sounds* in April 2022 ('a mish-mash...misfiring...so-so...flawed') but received the October 1972 material ('revelations...creative, catalytic') as if it unveiled a band that the released album had somehow chosen to obfuscate. In other words, the reviewer thought Nektar themselves lacked the discernment to properly conduct their own career.

And all because I reckon Nektar didn't have the gumption to actually make this a live album – in which case it would be remembered rapturously – or, at the very least, to graft on a wall of fake applause.

In actuality, the band were after the best of both worlds. They were aware that recording a live album would be problematic. We don't know of any early attempts to capture the live band professionally, though Brockett did run off tapes from the mixing board, but even if there were facilities available, they likely would not catch a perfect show. Indeed, the first time Nektar attempted to record live using the Pye Records mobile was on 6 November 1973, and that was a failure. They tried again 19 days later, meaning we got the infinitely hipper *Sunday Night at London Roundhouse* LP when it could easily have been *Tuesday Night at Yeovil Technical College*.

So they did the next best thing. They pulled a bunch of friends to the big room in Stommeln, loaded up on whatever looseners the occasion demanded, and played all their otherwise unrecorded pieces to them. The recordings were fierce and unadorned, single passes without overdubs or tampering. They then mastered the disc to the limit of what heavyweight 1973 vinyl could accommodate, pushing up the compression so that the needle practically blazes in the groove. This is not an album to denigrate for the excellence of its company, but to savour for the near-unprecedented punk-bettering verve of its creation: a white-hot band making a white-hot album in practically as much time as it takes to hear it.

All songs composed by Albrighton, Howden, Freeman, and Moore except where marked.

'Good Day'

Already a live favourite, 'Good Day' (or 'Good-Day', depending on which part of the sleeve you believe) was also the perfect opener for an album the band thought might introduce them to new fans. It's one of the more moderate tracks (at 6:46) without being poppy-short, and it's catchy without being too slavishly commercial. It heralds a band that can construct fine material with restraint but has enough scope for intricate prog changes and some exemplary instrumental dexterity. It also knows how to rock out, containing one of Albrighton's most furious solos. Additionally, its decision to roll in out of silence, much like Procol Harum's *Shine on Brightly*, suggests a band of monolithic stature caught mid-flow in an act that, for all we know, has been thundering on since the dawn of time. Catch *this*, that minute-long build-up claims – it's important.

Lyrically, the song is a moment of uplift in which the singer encounters himself in a mirror and is delighted by what he sees. Thus fortified, he steps confidently outward into the world – the title is actually a farewell. It's the antithesis of Albrighton's 'A Better Way' 40 years later when age has riven fissures in that bright morning face.

'New Day Dawning'

A more measured blues with touches of Deep Purple's 'Child in Time', this second waking-up song is the flip of the first. Morning, here, heralds nothing but pain and confusion, and even now, the night of death is close behind. The chorus is a despairing blast of Freeman's churchy organ chords and Albrighton's tortured vocal cries. There's another room-shredding solo before the band switch incongruously into an uncredited (and, somehow, unprosecuted) cover of The Beatles' 'Norwegian Wood', apparently for no reason other than that's what they habitually did when they performed the song live. We get only the first verse sung in harmony to Freeman's joyous organ blips before Albrighton's wah-wah scours us back to 'New Day Dawning'. It's nevertheless a polarising moment. Dropping into Beatles or other songs is so prog – it's what early Yes built their career on – but sounds laboured here, and very much old-fashioned in the wake of *Close to the Edge*.

'What Ya Gonna Do?'

Side one's closer begins as a Hendrix-style boogie before shifting to full-on breakneck electric blues in the style of Canned Heat and Ten Years After. Also known as 'Woman Trouble', it's merely five minutes of semi-coherent complaining about love, sex, and life in general – you're certainly not meant to attempt an analysis of the words. Freeman makes an enthusiastic fist of a rock'n'roll solo and continues to rollick engagingly behind Albrighton's storming guitar and manic scat-along. Moore lets loose on the bass, pile-driving the shuffle beat to a monstrous conclusion.

Hardly essential work, it does at least prove that Nektar could go neck-to-neck with the heaviest of them while retaining all the lightness of touch and warmth that bands such as Deep Purple had lost by 1973. For the only time, too, applause and chat at the end let us peek behind the curtain of the LP, though this revelation might have been better placed at the end of side four. 'What Ya Gonna Do?' has all the boisterous release of an encore, one last sweaty romp on the boards before the cold night air booms in.

'1-2-3-4'

The first of the album's epics (at 12:50), '1-2-3-4' damns with both its direct message and its furious marching rhythm. It comes on like a troop of soldiers all stamping forward together. Albrighton punctuates his own singing with angry squalls of guitar in much the same way as Hendrix's anti-war song 'Machine Gun', on which it was surely modelled. Freeman adds organ outrage that cuts even through this onslaught, and Moore's dark bass slurs like the ground-propagated shudder of distant explosions. Throughout, Howden's drumming is briskly military, propelling the listener against their will into the heart of the battle.

The piece was a triumph in live performance, and is here an early album peak. Had it been on a Hendrix LP, it would have been critically lauded as a career highlight. And as for legitimacy, well, Hendrix had merely served in the army during peacetime. Nektar lived, like those around them, in ruins still black with blood.

'Do You Believe in Magic?'

Young the band might be, but this was their third studio version of the song that has been released after the 1970 Boston session and the 1972 single. Nektar don't seem to have performed it in the original *Sounds* session in October 1972. It's a bouyant, informal reading, a band kicking back to enjoy themselves – and they do so with infectious verve, quickly dispensing with Albrighton's scat-accompanied solo for some huge Jon Lord organ chords, the point at which the single version ends.

The whole second half of its 7:20 running time is taken up with a dramatic coda which drags the listener through insipient mental breakdown to a scarifying guitar solo and a maelstrom of purest Purple proportions. What any of this has to do with the song's celebration of domesticity is beyond me – maybe the marriage didn't work out.

'Cast Your Fate'

Side three begins with this darkly sinuous song which alternates between stretches of brooding introspection and glimpses of desperate optimism, like a manic depressive's swiftly changing moods. Three minutes in, it abruptly lifts the pace for what seems to be misplaced enthusiasm, given the weariness with which the band thump at their instruments. A strident harmony vocal, half shouted, strains for stability in a storm, but the song remains opaque to the end, the singers incapable of expressing its ever-shifting core.

'A Day in the Life of a Preacher'

Just as 'Cast Your Fate' toiled for connection, so 'A Day in the Life of a Preacher' struggles to come into lyrical focus, finding its heart only toward the end when it switches to a eulogy for Jimi Hendrix, though even this is impossible to analyse based on the cryptic words alone (in one of his shouted asides, however, Albrighton does yell Jimi's name). The song seems to be constructed out of syllables chosen only to tick off the expected Nektar associations: blind man, madness, trying to hear me, death on the way, and so on. The likelihood is that it evolved onstage, like many early Nektar songs, and Albrighton's provisional, improvised words gradually become ossified into it. A building block, let's say, in search of a thematic album into which it could be revamped and slotted.

The original album suggests this 13:05 epic is a suite, giving the full title as 'A Day in the Life of a Preacher (Preacher) (Squeeze) (Mr. H)', but those three divisions are not consistently applied. They don't even appear on the inner sleeve, which prints the lyric. In live performance, when the piece took on ever more labyrinthine grandeur, other sections came and went, including long jams that greatly extended its duration. The October 1972 studio rendition even suggests that the song as presented here budded off from a version of 'Cast Your Fate'.

Onstage, Moore would introduce the song as being about 'a day in the life of a junkie'. He specifically means a needle user, the 'Mr. H' of the final part referring equally to Hendrix and heroin. But that adds nothing to make the bulk of the piece more comprehensible. Yes, you can get the thrust of 'Mr. H was a chiller', but Hendrix didn't die of heroin. He got drunk and swallowed too many barbiturates. Still, there's no incongruity about a band associated with psychedelics warning against the harder stuff. Since Bert Jansch's 'Needle of Death' in 1965, it had been a recurring theme in even the druggier reaches of rock.

'Preacher' begins the *Sounds* version with Man-style country swagger before abruptly switching to a more typical Nektar groove. Exactly the same effect would be used to introduce 'Show Me the Way' on *Down to Earth* the following year. It's good time, almost Faces-style heavy rock, tilting back and forth between tension and release to suggest everything's going to work out fine, regardless of our physical or mental troubles. The preacher here gets his sole reference as a man trying to right whatever ailments are afflicting the rest of society.

At 1:56, the band shift abruptly to a pummelling 15/8 rhythm over which Albrighton tortures his guitar until the notes give way to squeals of injured feedback – I assume this is 'Squeeze' since the word is mentioned in the lyric. The centre of this section is a rock workout, again highly reminiscent of Man at their most propulsive (say, in the jam parts of their Greasy Truckers version of 'Spunk Rock') featuring Freeman's Hammond.

At 6:42, we break into a slower instrumental bridge section (which may alternatively be 'Squeeze'), also Man-like, that gives Albrighton scope to make apocalyptic noises on his guitar. This resolves into what is definitely 'Mr. H' at 8:10, a direct, shockingly raw blues stomp highlighting Albrighton's playing at its most incendiary.

'Wings'

The brief 'Wings' starts the final side with a soaring power ballad sung in swirling three-part harmony. The lyric's evocation of floating through the sky, even though your body is stuck on the ground, prefigures *The Other Side* and may have been inspired by The Mandrake Memorial's 'Just a Blur' on the forgotten masterpiece *Puzzle* (1970), which expresses the same sentiment in similar words: 'even with my feet on the ground/my head would still be in the clouds' versus Nektar's 'my feet are on the ground/my head is all around'.

'Odyssee'

Like 'A Day in the Life of a Preacher', this monster of an album closer, the set's longest at 14:37, is also presented as a three-part suite on the cover: 'Odyssee (Ron's On) (Never, Never, Never) (Da-Da-Dum)' and grammatical variations thereof. However, I think it's actually in four parts, as we'll see. The informality of the titles – 'Ron's On' means that Howden gets to do his solo drum spot, and 'Da-Da-Dum' is simply an approximation of the beat – probably means the sections were intended as band identifiers rather than something to be presented to the record-buying public, though at least in this case they did make it to the lyric sheet. 'Odyssee' is, besides, a patchwork. Parts of the track could be woven into other constructs, and the 'Ron's On' feature added to just about any track that needed to give the other three musicians a break. Not Brockett, though: this was the point he really had to step up his lightshow to match Howden beat for beat. Coming here at the end, with a significantly different construction in the October 1972 version, it suggests a wrapping up of all the odds and ends that had not found a vehicle elsewhere on the disc.

Given the way the titles to 'A Day in the Life of a Preacher' were organised, you'd expect the first part to be 'Ron's On'. However, there's no Howden spotlight for more than five minutes. Instead, the suite kicks off as a spritely shuffle enabling Freeman to get in some jazzy chords and plucky finger runs. Very soon, all four musicians are dancing around each other until – you can pretty much sense the eye-to-eye signal – they fire up a monstrous ensemble riff that gives Albrighton the chance to exercise his wah-wah footwork. There's a section in which the singers all mutter at each other (Albrighton's snarling cry 'you'd better believe it!' is the only comprehensible line). Eventually, the rhythm collapses to feedback squall and disconnected bass and organ runs before Howden's frenetic drumming separates itself. All this work, I will assume, is actually a section titled 'Odyssee' given how the sections to the 'Cast Your Fate Jam' in the bonus tracks are organised.

Regardless of how the suite's labelled, it's 5:47 before Howden actually gets to fly solo for his 'Ron's On' spot, and when he does, it's to an unrelenting barrage of percussion that takes us headlong into the band's return a scant 65 seconds later – nothing here for drumophobes to complain about.

'Never, Never, Never' is an intense muted-strings workout over which Albrighton shouts the piece's first lyric, again most likely a chiselling into habit of some offhand words: the singer looks deeply at himself and decides he needs something to help him 'find my way out of this hell'. It, too, is swiftly dispatched at 8:51 for the monstrous riffs of 'Da-Da-Dum', no prisoners blues rock at a volume high enough to flap your speakers inside out. That all this energy was laid down in a studio, of all places, is testament to the band members knowing from their earlier session that they could pull off the trick, and indeed it's hard to imagine even the best of Nektar's live performances matching this ferocity and drive.

Alternate versions and bonus tracks

UA issued a promotional single in the UK in 1973 that paired the LP version of 'What Ya Gonna Do?' with the first five and a half minutes of 'A Day in the Life of a Preacher'.

The 2006 CD release on Dream Nebula Recordings includes a second disc of bonus material recorded at the original October 1972 session, complete with applause from the few people in the studio audience, and on 19 February 1973 ('Da Da Dum' and 'Wings'). The tracklist below is the corrected list given on the band's website. All this music appears on the CD, but not all of it is labelled there.

'Good Day'

The 1972 performance is far from shabby. It's raw, monstrous, and insanely intense. The problem is that Albrighton's in full-on rock god mode. His guitar dominates the mix to the point that whenever he lets rip, everything else is swallowed up in the onslaught, especially Freeman's rather cowed-sounding organ. Perhaps he was too drunk to figure out the amp and simply flicked all the knobs to full. The solo is merely a wall of noise, Hendrix so far into sonic meltdown he needs to be propped upright by a roadie.

'New Day Dawning'

As if played in a vast space rather than a studio, the loud sections of this 1972 version billow chaotically around the hollow of your head, making 'Norwegian Wood' still more of a chore to get through. Albrighton's over-saturated guitar is less focused than the *Sounds* version, and his solo is again a mess. It's like being trepanned with an angle grinder. There's a flub in the harmony vocal, and the band seem to struggle finding their way back to the refrain.

'Sunshine Down on the City'

It's easy to see why this relatively pedestrian rocker from the October 1972 session was passed over on *Sounds*, and it's not just the sour guitar sound that likely needed a tuning tweak. It simply never catches fire. In particular, Freeman finger-walks at the organ as if he's no longer sure what the keys are for. Is it too fanciful to propose that Freeman's state is what prompts Albrighton's laugh in the final verse? He does then manage a kind of Richard Wright bridge passage, perhaps with his nose.

The briefest snatch of the melody was later reworked into *Remember the Future,* but there's nothing else in the least memorable here.

'Saviour'
Nine minutes into 'Sunshine Down on the City', the band suddenly brighten it into this uncredited track, actually an earlier version of 'Preacher' with a variant lyric but one just as dispensable. They ride the groove, somewhat uncertainly, for a further four minutes while Freeman seeks the right note and clings on to it like he's drowning in a vat of liquid THC.

'Da Da Dum'
According to the CD, this section of 'Odyssee' was recorded at the same February 1973 sessions as the bulk of the finished album but is played standalone even though the band already had that unbeatable LP version of the suite in the can. It kicks off from a cold start, spanked into life by Albrighton's guitar, and this is likely the reason it never quite reaches the abandoned peaks of crazed riff overload of the full track.

'What Ya Gonna Do?'
Albrighton barely holds the opening blues riff together, causing another band member to clap him a beat. When he's finally in the groove, the others pound in, enabling him to shift to searing fuzz chords and angry flights of staccato notes. Freeman's feature is again a treat, as it would be on the 1973 version, though it's not easy to hear him through the roar. The heart of the performance, however, is a blues solo by Albrighton played with such intensity that the others wisely all step back to clear him room. It builds and builds, each bar more frenetic than the last, proving that the player could have wiped the floor with Alvin Lee and Richie Blackmore if he'd wanted, but Nektar wasn't that kind of band.

'It's All in Your Mind'
Another piece from October 1972 that was not revived for *Sounds*, it consists of a dreamy wah-wah feature accompanied only by Moore's delicate playing that alternates with vicious eruptions of muscular fuzz over a marching beat. The CD presents this and the next two tracks (uncredited) as a suite, but this song dies to silence after 4:33.

'Candlelight'
This second part (previously recorded in the Boston session) is storming hard rock set on a bed of Freeman's organ drones and chord runs. Albrighton attacks his guitar for a series of abusive, shapeless solos.

'I Can See You'

Emerging directly out of 'Candlelight', this would, of course, later be integrated into *Remember the Future* – both melody and lyric are already in place. Disappointingly, it fades during the line 'bluebird, what do you feel?' And yes, Albrighton *does* sing 'bluebird', even this early.

'Mr. H'

The October 1972 rendition of the piece is listed on the CD as 'Cast Your Fate Jam' but actually consists of a suite consisting of 'Mr. H', 'Cast Your Fate', 'Odyssee', and the drum solo 'Ron's On'. There may well have been more planned, but that's where we leave the tape: a punishing 20:26 of unrelenting heavy rock propulsion.

Kicking things off, 'Mr. H' is complete as far as its melodic changes go, but at this point appears to lack a lyric, regardless that the band claim it was written in response to Hendrix's death back in 1970. Instead, Albrighton scats some placeholder vocals and fills the space with guitar solos. Surely if there *were* words, he would have used them.

'Cast Your Fate Jam'

At 5:06, it shifts to the 'Cast Your Fate' rhythm, to which somebody (not a member of the band) claps along. Again the words are lacking, but Albrighton occupies the verses with improvised phrases – the refrain is 'when will it end?'

'Odyssee'

A drum smash at 10:56 pushes the band into the jazzy shuffle familiar from the LP version, which, as I mentioned earlier, is likely an unlabelled section under the suite title since it's presented that way here, according to the band's website.

It romps gleefully through its changes, including the muttered vocals section culminating in Albrighton's 'you'd better believe it!'

'Ron's On' (Howden)

Howden's drum apocalypse erupts out of the wreckage of 'Odyssee' at 17:03, and the band drop away shortly after. This is a much more substantial solo, weaving its way through a series of patterns and tempo shifts for more than three minutes, always seemingly on the verge of collapse before coming to an abrupt halt into applause.

'Wings'

The February 1973 studio version is played faster and cleaner but with less engagement and not so rich a harmony, though Albrighton's lead vocal is at his throat-shredding best.

The 2013 CD release on Purple Pyramid includes promo edits of the LP versions of '1-2-3-4' and 'Do You Believe In Magic?' (*not* from the 1972 single). It also includes a second disc of the parts of the album that were played live in Darmstadt on 13 November 1971. For more on this concert, see the Live Recordings chapter at the end of this book.

Remember the Future (1973)

Personnel:
Roye Albrighton: guitar, lead vocals
Allan 'Taff' Freeman: keyboards, vocals
Ron Howden: drums, vocals
Derek 'Mo' Moore: bass, vocals
Recorded: August 1973 at Chipping Norton Recording Studios, England
Producers: Nektar, Peter Hauke
Released: Bacillus Records LP, November 1973 (West Germany)
Running time: 35:29 (A: 16:34 B: 18:55)

Imagine this: it's 1973, the very pinnacle of rock's reach, ingenuity, and ambition. You're one of the biggest bands in the country, and you're gigging constantly. It's your busiest time ever, with a major tour booked just ahead supporting Frank Zappa's *Over-Nite Sensation* band across Europe. You've released four discs worth of inventive, original music in the past two years. The most recent came out little over three months ago. Nevertheless, you head into the studio in the tiny window available to you before the tour commences, armed with only a basic plan for what you're going to do. A week later, you emerge with one of the finest albums ever recorded.

If *Remember the Future* didn't take Nektar by surprise – the music, I mean, not its success – then it should have. The album was a leap forward both in terms of its technical surety and the melodic ease with which the band filled the vinyl. It all but dances from start to finish, a series of tumbling riffs and funky breaks that never seem weighty or laboured. It was a single 35-minute piece of music that felt as if it all belonged together – no chaotic shifting from idea to idea like *Journey to the Centre of the Eye* or patchwork of fragments like 'A Tab In The Ocean' – and, almost uniquely among prog rock of the time, seemed to have poured out effortlessly. All the band needed to do was channel it onto tape. You never get the feeling that the album was hard work to create and consequently it's never hard work to hear.

While the music fell into place naturally, the lyric feels somewhat underdeveloped. For all the strength of their music, Nektar never seemed primarily interested in the conventions of songwriting, and their lyrics were generally sparse, perfunctory, even downright meaningless. Where they expressed a story as on *Journey,* that story was recounted mostly through sound. The lyrics sometimes seem bolted on, the weakest part of their skill. The words are rarely memorable, the imagery rarely compelling. There's certainly the case that if you attempt to unravel *Remember* without its inner gatefold note to guide you, you're going to get nowhere with it – the whole album might as well be in German.

Jethro Tull is a good reference point for those approaching *Remember*, simply because you're likely already familiar with the band's two comparable

47

epics. Nektar may well have been, too: *Thick as a Brick* was released the previous year, *A Passion Play* this March.

Navigating *Thick* musically is simple enough because the tunes are strong and the album shifts gears slickly from motif to motif. Its only hiccup is that sudden change of tempo near the end of the second side. But despite the vast amount of text on the multi-page album cover, Ian Anderson never attempted to explain the lyric, and by themselves, the words are incomprehensible. I get glimpses of what they might mean, but I couldn't actually describe a credible story to you. *A Passion Play* is the opposite: the music is jerky and difficult, as if Anderson was challenging you to accommodate it, whereas the lyric tells a straightforward tale that is easy to follow from start to end. A man dies, he's taken on a journey of judgment through his own life, he ends up in hell, and he's redeemed. The album ends with his resurrected body hailing old friends – and it fades away just before we register their shock!

Remember falls somewhere between the two. It *does* have a story, but you'll have to extrapolate for yourself what that story means from an inadequate outline and gnomic words.

If you're new to the piece, you may be lucky enough to have an instant handle into it. There are labelled subdivisions, which I use below in my discussion of the album, that help you break it into navigable components. But these have not been added to every release and they were not present on the original 1973 LP. The initial release on Bacillus in West Germany and UA in the UK simply labelled the sides 'Part I' and 'Part II' on the inner gatefold and 'Part 1' and 'Part 2' on the labels. The gatefold printed all the lyrics for each side in a single vertical block. It was only in the US and Canada, when the album was finally issued there on Passport Records in 1974 (Nektar's first release in the continent), that each side gained its run of subdivisions, four in 'Part I' and six in 'Part II'. Issues in other territories continued to ignore them. They were not present on any CD release of the album until the 2014 Purple Pyramid three-disc set, but even then, the divisions were not indexed on the disc itself, so you still have to figure out for yourself where they all start and end.

So what's it about? From the gatefold, and from what little the band have ever said on the subject, I can glean the following:

In a back story, we learn that an alien called bluebird (the lyrics as presented in the gatefold write it consistently without a capital letter), apparently male, has made numerous trips to Earth before, but his appearance ('his blue skin and wings') is either hideous or frightening to humans. Perhaps it's simply obvious that he's some kind of extraterrestrial rather than that he might be, let's say, one of Arthur C. Clarke's devils. The story notes that humans 'either ran away from him or tried to harm him.' Either way, bluebird has found in us a primitive and hostile race, so it's a wonder he keeps returning. The reason he *does* will be made clear later.

Eventually, he makes telepathic contact ('bbbbrain to bbbbrain' as Daevid Allen said in *The Flying Teapot*, released three months before sessions began) with an unnamed blind boy, in other words, somebody who is incapable of seeing him and therefore is able to befriend him without judgement. The alien feeds images into the boy's mind, likely the first visuals he has ever seen – this is where Part I begins.

In the first section, 'Images of the Past', the alien shows the boy the entire span of life on Earth, a bit like the Moody Blues song 'Procession' from the 1971 album *Every Good Boy Deserves Favour* (the one with the old man imparting wisdom to a young boy on the cover), from the first fish to heave itself out of the water to man inventing the wheel. This links into the fittingly titled 'Wheel of Time', which explains that bluebird has witnessed all human history himself but has never been able to intervene. He must simply watch whatever mankind chooses to do. In 'Remember the Future' itself, bluebird intimates that he is able to see into the future, too, and that the boy is not to be concerned about it – great things lie ahead. The side concludes with 'Confusion,' an instrumental summary of the boy's feelings at the end of all this.

Throughout, there's a strong spiritual subtext to bluebird's lecture. Even though the alien has seen evolution at work, he describes time as being like dead leaves 'falling down from heaven.' Mankind is just as warlike in *Remember* as in *Journey*, but here at least, the species is capable of redemption, unlike the thoroughly depressing earlier album. Bluebird claims that even in our most aggressive moods, we are 'blessed' and that war is necessary so that mankind can 'make good their rights.' More perplexingly, bluebird mentions someone or something named 'rainbow', but the inference is surely that of the Biblical flood and a new covenant never to attempt to destroy humanity again, no matter how disobedient or evil the species becomes. Finally, Part I repeatedly has bluebird ask the question, 'who made you and me?' not so much as an admission that there are secrets not even this omnipotent angelic telepathic alien can unlock, but as a means of getting the boy to figure out the truth for himself.

Part I has all been one-sided, a sermon from the stars, but in Part II we gain a voice. After bluebird grants the boy the gift of sight in 'Returning Light', the kid seems to recognise him as a divine creature himself. As the story puts it: 'the boy realises now who his friend is.' In fact, given what is about to happen, he is most surely an avatar of Christ.

In 'Questions and Answers', the boy enters into a dialogue with bluebird in which he receives 'wisdom' regarding everything he ever wanted to know. Thus enlightened, the boy himself expresses his new knowledge in 'Tomorrow Never Comes', which consists of aphorisms or proverbs of unity and love: 'smile if you want to, not when you can.' But the mood darkens in the pointedly titled 'Path of Light' when bluebird explains what he knows of his *own* future: to walk a lonely road, and eventually to be crucified.

Like actors on a stage – let's say *Hair*, since Albrighton was part of the London orchestra for that show before joining Prophecy – who suddenly connect, boy and bluebird gaze into each other's eyes in 'Recognition', fusing preacher and disciple into one accord. The album ends with a hymn to ecology, 'Let it Grow', in which the alien gives an ultimate warning: nature is there to 'heal' mankind, but if we damage nature, not even bluebird himself will come to save us. The 'it' in the title is the planet's plants and animals, the love and respect in our hearts, and the soul that guides us. Then bluebird departs back into the heavens, and the boy begins his ministry on Earth.

Heavy stuff. You can understand why it made sense to couch all this new age Christian didacticism in the same science fiction trappings as the earlier *Journey*, which was no less an exhortation. As I mentioned earlier, Daevid Allen knew in his own space sermon *Radio Gnome Invisible* that the best way to impart a spiritual message is to package it in a frothy disguise. Allen hid it with humour, Nektar with bubbly rock that slips down the throat as sweet as, well, honey.

You don't have to agree with this reading. You certainly don't have to think that *Remember the Future* is religious moralising that you must heed any more than you heed the religious moralising of *Radio Gnome Invisible*. My feeling is that *Remember* is heartfelt, in the same way that Magma's spirituality was heartfelt, but that it makes no difference. Christian Vander disguised his own spiritual message in an invented language. He turned the sermon literally into incomprehensible syllables on classic third album *Mekanïk Destruktïẁ Kommandöh*, released the same month as *The Flying Teapot*. Nektar's continuity of thought moves seamlessly from *Journey* (repent of war or we will all die) to *Remember* (find balance with nature or we will all die) and on to *Recycled* (cease abusing the environment or we will all die). But I suspect they didn't want to labour the listener. The obvious antecedent for *Remember* is The Who's *Tommy*, in which, just like *Remember*, a disabled boy finds God, his senses are restored, and he begins preaching the revelations he'd gained. But *Tommy* bashes you over the head with this message until you're sick of it. Nektar certainly did not intend to do the same.

And you don't have to know the story or take its teaching to heart to enjoy *Remember the Future*. Whatever your religious beliefs, simply in isolation – judging lines and verses merely by themselves – the words can be deeply moving, especially since Albrighton sings them with such feeling. It's the same way that a Jon Anderson lyric can drive you to tears in one of Yes's grand spiritual albums without you actually caring what it means. *Tales from Topographic Oceans*, released the month after *Remember*, is impenetrable gobbledygook apparently based on Hindu scripture (Jon Anderson admitted that he tended to choose words for their sound, not for their meaning), but it raises and lowers the spirits like an obedient yoyo, and that's all it ever needs to do.

Suffice it to say that *Remember* was written as a single piece and intended as a story and a message. Nektar managed to work in various snippets of existing songs and musical ideas and changes that the members had toyed with during their recent tours, laying the entire backing track down on their first day in Chipping Norton. In a 2021 conversation with *VWMusic*, Moore remembered: 'We wrote most of the lyrics in the studio as Mick [Brockett] and I pieced the story of the album together.' During three further marathon sessions, the band overdubbed and added vocals.

There was even a preliminary mix at CBS Studios in Whitfield Street, London, for what was intended from the start to be primarily a quadraphonic release. Nektar then headed off for its high-profile tour supporting The Mothers Of Invention (Zappa's last with Jean-Luc Ponty) that took it from Copenhagen on 18 August to the Empire Pool in Wembley, London on 14 September. I count just seven days off, never more than one at a time, between the gigs on this frantic, wide-ranging tour, but still, it seems that at some point during the tour, the band realised that the CBS Studios mix was faulty and needed to be done over. 'The speakers were out of phase,' Moore told *VWMusic*, 'and the guitar on that version almost disappeared.' So sometime, somehow, in the midst of the tour, Albrighton and Moore rushed the tapes over to Stommeln, where the final quad and stereo mixes were achieved.

Swift, giddy, almost carelessly impetuous work. It doesn't fit the contemporary paradigm of dinosaur bands wasting months in the studio, but it's closer to the truth. Long LP sessions, like the 51 days it took to record *The Dark Side of the Moon*, in three blocks spaced months apart, were still the exception in 1973. Many of our golden age classics were hurried onto tape in a single week snatched out of a touring schedule.

The album was released in November to a rapturous response in West Germany. The band seemed to know from the start that they had a special event on their hands. Albrighton enthused to *It's Psychedelic Baby* in 2012 about how 'something magical' happened in the studio. He told *Something Else!* the same year:

It was a very good album, and one that I really enjoyed making along with the other guys in the band. I believe that that album put Nektar in a class of its own, away from the Genesis/Yes/Gentle Giant school.

He had a right to distance himself from British prog, given that the LP managed only muted regard in the UK – it did not even chart there.

As for the US, attempts to even find a *label* for the band in America dragged on for years, with Zappa himself having shown the greatest interest. Finally, in 1974, Passport Records took a punt on the band. Passport was a new imprint set up by the Jem Records import business, which that same year tried to tickle the US with European albums such as Robert Calvert's *Captain Lockheed and the Starfighters* (good luck with *that!*), Camel's *Mirage*, Capability Brown's *Voice*, Lucifer's Friend's highly underrated *Banquet*, and Tangerine Dream's *Phaedra*. It was also home to Larry Fast's Synergy and prog band Fireballet (featuring Ryche Chlanda on guitar), about whom more later. You might have hoped Camel, at least, would gain some notice, but *Mirage* struggled in the US, climbing no higher than 149 on the *Billboard* chart. Were there hopes at all, I wonder, when Passport put out the more daunting, less approachable *Remember the Future* in June?

But the miraculous happened: stations spun the promo edits, listeners liked what they heard and the disc began to sell in large quantities. *Remember* entered *Billboard* at 190 in the week beginning 20 July, climbing ten places the following week, ten more the week after. Slowly and surely, it continued to ascend. By the end of August, it was at 122 and Nektar were flinging their amps and projectors on a plane to tour the country.

The appearances shoved the album skyward. *Remember* breached the top 100 on 21 September, overtook Triumvirat's *Illusions on a Double Dimple* on 12 October, bested that album's highest showing (55) the week after, and hit its peak of 19 for two weeks on 16 November. Only Jethro Tull's *War Child* hoisted the prog flag higher that month.

Later, Albrighton tried to explain the album's success. He told *Get Ready to Rock* in 2008:

> We never went out of our way to write a specific type of music for any of our albums. It just came out as it did. Being as *Remember the Future* was the first release in the USA and got the push it did, this is probably the reason it did so well. I think the same could have happened to *A Tab in the Ocean* if that had been the first.

And *Sea of Tranquility* in 2011:

> If you were to look at the charts in those early 1970s, above and below us were acts that were totally different from Nektar's music. We kind of stuck out like a sore thumb, which made people sit up and listen.

Remember didn't leave the chart until the end of January 1975, by which time Nektar were selling out venues across the East Coast and there was a quite different import album in the racks to assimilate.

All songs composed by Albrighton, Howden, Freeman, and Moore.

'Remember the Future Part I'

Satisfyingly unified it may seem, but *Remember the Future* actually has less structure than 'A Tab in the Ocean', which sandwiches its extemporisations in true jazz fashion between iterations of a theme. *Remember* is a bunch of different sections all joined together without any attempt to reintroduce motifs you've heard before, or to wrap everything up neatly – so long as they flow one to another nicely, that's enough. *Thick as a Brick* and *A Passion Play* both returned to where they started. Even *The Dark Side of the Moon*, ostensibly also a series of sections without structure, has a refrain, it's simply cunningly disguised so that the band couldn't be accused of labouring it as they had in 'Atom Heart Mother'. There are three iterations of the 'Breathe' theme spaced across the disc, the third hiding behind the title 'Any Colour You Like'. It's also unified by a heartbeat effect. But heading off somewhere and never coming back was not a weakness in a conceptual album, given that Mike Oldfield's one-track disc *Tubular Bells* (released that May) was merely a bolted-together collage of components without a unifying theme, and that went on to sell millions.

I'd wager that feel is more important than motif. The prog fan may ask themselves whether 'Supper's Ready' is a better epic than 'A Plague of Lighthouse Keepers' because it reprises its theme. I'd give 'Plague' the nod, personally, and hence argue that the reprise is unnecessary. It's neat to know that the end is on the way, which is why there's a convention in movies to reprise something from the opening just before the final act, but it doesn't damage the experience if that reprise is omitted. 'A Plague of Lighthouse Keepers' is unified by its singular and distinctive sound world, which is maintained from start to end, and the same is true of *Remember*. Albrighton said as much in the 2011 CD booklet:

> In the studio, in the corner was a Hammond organ and a Leslie cabinet and we thought about plugging in the guitar. [Which] was great, as this was the glue that went through the entire piece.

The various fragments of *Remember* are bonded not just by Albrighton's quavery guitar glue but by all the other components of the band's particular sonic landscape that we now recognise as the quintessential Nektar sound, including the conceptual continuity of the lyrical themes that I mentioned in the opening of this book.

There are, of course, dangers as well as advantages to having identifiable tropes, particularly when they solidify into heritage, something I'll come onto much later. New Nektar's 2018 album *Megalomania* includes the phrase 'take a trip back in time', and that sure wasn't coincidence.

The basic flow of 'Part I' is as follows: a tinkling introduction with ominous drone leads into the first of the album's weightless soap bubble guitar grooves. 'Images of the Past' (running 2:15) is the album's first self-contained song, a quick-stepping soft funk with an instantly catchy melody. It's fun, incidentally, to hear the band sing the refrain 'evolution' with US pronunciation rather than their native British. An ear on that market, perhaps, already? It shifts through an instrumental bridge (1:04) with a shiny Leslie guitar riff to drop into the second song, 'Wheel of Time' (4:25), a soulful ballad with a glorious soaring chorus.

The next shift takes us to the third song, 'Remember the Future' (running 4:51 to the point it fades out of audibility), marked by its forceful title phrase that punctuates the section. This cross-fades into 'Confusion' (running 3:34 from the point the previous section fades away), a frantic 10/8 rhythm over which Albrighton lets rip on a punishing overdriven fuzz guitar solo. It subsides into a 3/4 romp toward the end and hangs the album side open on a final ringing guitar note.

'Remember the Future Part II'
'Returning Light' (running 1:45) opens the side: a slow, melancholy pawing out of darkness steeped in unresolved tension – like the boy, already maddened in 'Confusion', now on the verge of full-on hysteria. And indeed, it shifts abruptly to an anthemic guitar riff and a corkscrew ensemble piece that bursts into silence at the peak of its climb. It's hardly a song since there are only two lines ('I can see you/I can hear you') sung in Moody Blues harmony.

After a serene, stately introduction (1:13), the fourth song, 'Questions and Answers' (3:25), is buoyant stadium-filling pop, deepening majestically for the sections in which bluebird responds to the boy's wonder-filled enquiries with stricken cries of his own inability to change the fate of the world. An emotionally charged choral bridge (1:18) jolts abruptly into the more urgent rhythm of the fifth song 'Tomorrow Never Comes' (1:19). In the album's cleverest lyric, the boy claims that there's infinite possibility for laughter and tears since the future hasn't been written yet, whereas bluebird retorts that the future is simply a past we haven't yet experienced, and hence nothing can deflect a person from their fate. Indeed, this is heady stuff to be imparted in just nine lines, particularly since the fact that both boy and bluebird end their argument with the same triumphal tune demonstrates how the latter matches and then trumps the first.

Having thus expressed the inevitability of his demise, bluebird's monologue in the sixth song, 'Path of Light' (1:55), is achingly sad blues highlighting Freeman's very welcome Hammond drones and lifted by a spare guitar solo alternating between two quite different voicings. This is followed by the impassioned section 'Recognition' (2:24): a backwards echo of bluebird's coming pain. It's not really a song since there are minimal vocals, but it culminates in Albrighton's second huge-voiced eruption of fuzz, this time as elegantly sculpted as the most iconic David Gilmour solo.

The seventh and final song, 'Let it Grow' (5:09), shifts despair back into joy through an irresistible funky rhythm and some of Albrighton's best soul stylings. Both funk and soul are piled up to absurd degrees when the song shifts twice, first to a pounding sequence of gobbling wah-wah and Albrighton's best discothèque moves ('you know that I can't stop it!'), then to a full-on funk rock blast shouted in unison by Howden, Moore, and Freeman.

Finally, the album blows itself apart for 27 seconds of disconnected meltdown and, just as it fades, the voice of an English radio DJ sounding an awful lot like Jimmy Young, whom Pink Floyd had parodied on the tape that became 'One of These Days'. What's the DJ for? Unlike the Floyd, Nektar weren't known for their sonic jokes so there must be a point to this. Perhaps it's merely to note that life goes on, as banal as ever, heedless of the drama we've just lived through.

Alternate versions and bonus tracks

Navigating all the reissues of *Remember* is a nightmare, but let's try to make sense of them here. Excuse me if I miss anything significant.

The original Bacillus LP release was in quadraphonic. This mix has never been available on CD. However, the quad was upmixed to 5.1 in 2004 alongside the other period quad mixes (see more below). An eight-minute edit of the quad was placed on Bellaphon's quadraphonic sampler *The Fantastic World of Quadro* in 1973, alongside Dzyan, Nine Days Wonder, and some jazz artists. This is also unavailable elsewhere.

When it came time to issue the album on CD during the great silver disc gold rush in 1987, Bacillus erroneously used the faulty CBS Studios mix rather than the Dierks Studios remix. This rejected mix was used on every subsequent CD release – you'll know it by the lack of guitars – and was only corrected for the 2002 CD release on Bacillus. The correct mix has been used ever since.

Back in 1973, Bellaphon enabled West German radio stations to advertise the album with a promo single of excerpts. Both sides were simply labelled 'Remember the Future' on that disc, but they were given titles for Bacillus's 2002 CD. They were also released on a 2006 Japanese mini-LP sleeve CD of the album on WHD Entertainment and included as a bonus vinyl single in a 2011 LP version on Sireena Records.

The more substantial, listed as 'Lonely Roads', is a straight transcription of 'Path of Light' with a cold open shortly before the vocal 'walking down lonely roads'. It fades during the guitar solo 3:50 later. The other, 'Let It Grow', is simply the last 2:18 of the album, again with a cold open.

The 2004 SACD release on Dream Nebula Recordings also includes these two excerpts. Additionally, it includes an edit created for a 2001 compilation on ZYX Music called *Made in Germany Vol. 2* (alongside the likes of Guru Guru, Kraan, Mythos, and Wallenstein) and the entire album remixed into 5.1. There was also a CD version with the bonus tracks but omitting the 5.1 layer.

The *Made in Germany* edit runs 9:51 and is simply a cunning amalgam of highlights as follows. It begins with a cold open on the bubbly guitar 0:26 seconds into 'Part I' and follows through the Part until 3:12 (all these timings are from the full LP), when it omits a short section, smash-cutting instead to 3:27. From here it runs to 3:46 and leaps forward on another splice to 10:16 (just before the line 'and now that you've seen me'). It trims a few short sections out of the driving instrumental and fades away at about 12:57. 'Part II' is crossfaded into this, picking up the Part at about 13:28 shortly before 'I can see you through the morning mist.' The rest of the album is then reproduced verbatim except for one trim to excise the repeat of the 'you know that I can't stop it!' sequence.

To promote *Remember the Future* in the US, Passport issued a single to radio stations in 1974, pairing 'Remember the Future' (3:30) with 'Confusion' (3:43). These are the two sections at the end of Part I. To my knowledge, these edits have never been released on CD.

The 2011 CD release on ItsAboutMusic includes a second disc it labels 'Vivo Niteroi (Live in Brazil)' and dates to 2007. This is actually the concert recorded at Teatro Municipal in Niterói, Brazil, on 10 November 2005. It is not presented in its correct order. The live performance of the full *Remember* suite is placed at the end of the first disc (confusingly, not even labelled as being from Brazil) and the rest on the second disc. For more on this concert, see the Live Recordings chapter at the end of this book.

The 2013 CD release on Purple Pyramid includes a second disc comprising the three bonus tracks from the 2004 Dream Nebula Recordings version, plus what it here labels *The 1970 Boston Tapes*. The *Made in Germany* edit is here wrongly labelled a 'radio edit'. The following year Purple Pyramid released the same double CD set *again*, but this time in a limited deluxe edition with a reticular cover and sew-on patch plus a third disc comprising the entire *Unidentified Flying Abstract* album, even though every fan worth their salt had already owned that for 12 years. Still: reticular, patch – bargain. For more on the Boston and *Abstract* releases, see the Other Studio Recordings chapter at the end of this book.

Also in 2014 (and it *was* the album's 41st anniversary, after all) Purple Pyramid released it as a double CD set consisting of the album alone (no bonus tracks) and a second disc of highlights from the Academy Of Music concert on 28 September 1974 that had already been released in full as the *Live in New York* double CD in 2004.

Down to Earth (1974)

Personnel:
Roye Albrighton: guitar, lead vocals
Allan 'Taff' Freeman: keyboards, vocals
Ron Howden: drums, vocals
Derek 'Mo' Moore: bass, vocals
Additional personnel (in order of appearance):
Phil Brown, Stephan Wick: tuba on 'Astral Man'
Robert Calvert: ringmaster's announcements
Ron Carthy, Steve Gregory, Butch Hudson, Chris Mercer, Chris Pyne: brass and
sax section on 'Nelly the Elephant,' 'Fidgety Queen,' 'Oh Willy,' 'Finale'
P. P. Arnold, Kenneth Cole: vocals on 'Early Morning Clown,' 'That's Life,' 'Little
Boy'
Recorded: March to April 1974 at Chipping Norton Recording Studios, England
Producers: Peter Hauke, Nektar
Released: Bacillus Records LP, October 1974 (West Germany)
Running time: 37:04 (A: 18:21 B: 18:43)

Nektar have expressed ambivalence about this album. The consensus seems
to be that the band would have become stratospheric had they followed
Remember the Future directly with *Recycled*. A typical reaction is the one
Albrighton gave to *Progressive Ears* in 2004:

> Back in the 1970s, the Germans knew that every time we did something, it
> would be different, so they went and bought it. You have to be careful here
> [in the US]. We came out with [*Down to Earth*] after *Remember the Future*,
> and I'm not sure the American public were ready for that because it was a
> totally different thing.

You can imagine how the ideal timeline would work: given the delay between
Nektar recording their albums and their release in the US, *Recycled* would
have been primed and ready to go by the time the band began their tours in
support of *Remember*. It could have been released to fanfares and triumph in
the middle of 1975. More and even greater successes were sure to follow.

But this is revisionism. When Nektar recorded *Remember,* they had no
inkling as to its fate in North America. They *still* had no inkling as to its
fate when they recorded *Down to Earth* in spring 1974 – well ahead of the
previous album's release there. *Down to Earth* was certainly not written
with the US in mind. Its quirky, humorous, defiantly delinquent attitude –
blockhead thrills and sawdust deviance – was utterly unsuited to that market.
It was meant for West Germany, perhaps even a parody of what Nektar
thought they had to sound like to break Britain. Though it actually did do
good business in the US, reaching all of 32 in *Billboard* and spawning the
closest Nektar ever had to a hit single. My suspicion is that it coasted on

the previous album's success – it tends to be the album *after* the classic that charts with a bullet, since the audience rush out to buy it upon release – and the result was actually to fuddle the market.

Nektar's ultimate failure in the US is generally blamed on *Recycled*. But *Recycled* was exactly what the market wanted next. I think *Down to Earth* put the band in a perplexing place, a slippery European act without a pigeonhole, part comedy, part earnest philosophising, from which they could never have recovered.

But there it is, stuck awkwardly in the midst of the band's golden age. And despite all of its problems, *Down to Earth* is still highly regarded by fans. It certainly does grow on you. I hated it the first few times I tried to play it. Now I simply roll with the Pythonesque absurdity of the piece. (I use that word knowingly: Python was also a Circus.) Moreover, its shift toward shorter, more commercial songs did light a way forward, and a couple of those songs have become fan favourites even if they're never likely to top a poll of Nektar highlights.

As usual, the album began with isolated fragments and songs that this incorrigibly creative band had worked up during rehearsal sessions and sound checks. They soon hit on a circus theme, which in effect, merely meant a few new songs and the judicious rewriting of the existing material to match the concept. Much of *Down to Earth* actually doesn't evoke a circus at all. Albrighton wrote in the only CD liner notes the album has ever warranted:

> One of the tunes that we had been playing around with over the months at sound checks was a heavy stomping riff which reminded us all of a herd of elephants. I guess this...eventually led to the circus idea.

Why a *circus,* of all things? The idea was old enough to be a cliché. There was one obvious antecedent – the Rolling Stones' ill-fated *Rock and Roll Circus* in December 1968 – but the idea of merging rock with circus was common currency even by then. Pink Floyd had expressed their intention to perform in a circus tent as early as 1967, the year of John Lennon's 'Being for the Benefit of Mr. Kite': 'We'll have a huge tent and go around like a travelling circus...we'll have a huge screen, 120 feet wide and 40 feet high inside, and project films and slides' Roger Waters told *Melody Maker* that August. They were still expressing this intention as late as *The Wall*, which they originally wanted to stage inside a giant worm-shaped tent.

Nektar hadn't played Circus Krone's big top in Munich during their Mothers Of Invention tour, but the place was a touring hotspot: Mahavishnu Orchestra, The Moody Blues, King Crimson, and Uriah Heep all performed there in the months before the band started work on their circus album. Nektar (who posed there among its performers for the inner gatefold) would finally play the venue in October 1975, Zappa a few years later. Pink Floyd played

Circus Krone in 1970 and headlined the Amsterdam Rock Circus in May 1972 alongside Santana and Donovan.

Many had tried a circus or carnival theme. Many more would try. To give just a few examples: There were British prog rock bands called Circus (Mel Collins was a member) and Cirkus, an Italian band called Circus 2000, and another Circus from Switzerland that hadn't released an album yet. The Doors and Family put circus performers on their LP covers. Gong's second album was the soundtrack to the motorbike racing movie *Continental Circus*. The nightclub Electric Circus in New York opened in 1967, and staged circus acts between bands. Can performed in 1972 with circus-style variety acts. *Circus* was one of the biggest American rock music magazines, taking that name in 1969. Procol Harum's genre-defining 'In Held Twas in I' included a trip through the circus of the soul, as did Van der Graaf Generator's 'A Plague of Lighthouse Keepers'. Mick Brockett's lightshow business was called Fantasia Light Circus. The Hammond organ, played with jaunty pomp, naturally evokes disreputable big top showbiz – witness, for example, its use on 'Richard Lionheart' on *Monument* (1967) by Hansson & Karlsson (themselves no stranger to the European K!). In the same year as *Down to Earth,* Ronnie Lane toured with his own version, inviting Vivian Stanshall as ringmaster. Bob Dylan staged a revue the following year, his face caked up in clown's white.

And so on and so on. Almost none of rock's attempts to evoke the edgy excitement of a circus actually worked. And yet Nektar thought they could breathe life into the theme. The idea was that the band had gone too far into space already and it was time to taste the dirt. *Down to Earth* would be an album utterly grounded in the mundane, without a hint of psychedelia's open cosmos or prog's airy pretensions. It would be animal-scented and tactile. It would deal with ordinary people, the same dreams of stardom and fears of failure among the jumbled refuse of mainstream society that had fuelled movies ever since *Freaks* and *Nightmare Alley*. More so even than the outcast boy in *Remember, Down to Earth* would celebrate our small, haunted, lonely lives, and it would commiserate with us when we fell, figuratively, with all the bone-jarring impact of the man whose foot slips on the high wire.

A comedown, then, a deliberate turning of the back on the ethereal, just as Pink Floyd had expressed on *The Dark Side of the Moon*. And yes, there *was* a progress forward. *Recycled*, too, eschewed space for our own polluted planet. What's more, *Down to Earth* was an album of connection, to the extent of putting the band on the front cover, and connection was the theme of *Remember,* just as it had been the theme in Pink Floyd since *Meddle*. We are the performers, you are the audience, but there's actually no difference between us, and it's time to bridge the gap.

This new sense of community stretched even to the recording sessions. Undoubtedly using a British studio helped to gather in the guests. A brass section added parping, distinctly earthbound noises. P. P. Arnold – the soul belter best known in prog circles for having sung with the Small Faces and Nick Drake, played with a pre-Yes Steve Howe, and incubated the Nice – added vocals on a few tracks, though she's almost unrecognisable as a celebrity voice. And fellow UA signing Robert Calvert came down to terrorise the village with his sword and aviator's helmet and act as the circus's ringmaster, though he's featured on only a few tracks and is abandoned altogether after the opening of the second side.

According to Albrighton in the *Retrospektive 1969–1980* booklet, Hawkwind were also in the studio at the time, so the band borrowed Calvert. This is odd: Hawkwind *were* recording *Hall of the Mountain Grill* at the time, but not in Chipping Norton. Besides, Calvert had left Hawkwind to focus on his solo career. He finished recording *Captain Lockheed and the Starfighters* in January. Still, Calvert *did* turn up (by Intercity train, seemingly, though Chipping Norton doesn't have a station of its own) and recited his parts with his usual ebullience. Some lines are plainly scripted, while others enabled crazy improvisation. Calvert's suggestion that listeners might want to indulge in 'experimental surgery' during the intermission of the LP flip must have gone down well in West Germany, particularly when declaimed in the same mock-German accent he'd used on the *Captain Lockheed* skits.

Later, when mixing the album once again in Stommeln, Dieter Dierks added 'special effects and sounds', likely some of the sonic uplift that means the album has not quite given up on evoking an expansive head space. Like its predecessor, it was mixed for quadraphonic, but no multi-channel version has ever been released on CD.

All songs composed by Albrighton, Howden, Freeman, and Moore.

'Astral Man'
Twenty seconds of circus sound effects hurry us in, then the band erupt into a comical galloping rhythm that does indeed sound like the house band pumping away on its platform, and a ringmaster bounding across the ring on legs tall as stilts. In particular, the tubas add a ridiculous low end like the elephants, awaiting their turn next on the schedule, shoving against the side of the tent to catch a peek. It's music straight out of *Dumbo* and that's about as deep as it plans to get. But 'Astral Man' is also insanely catchy, and its soaring refrains poignantly mirror the man on the tightrope hovering precariously over disaster, as are we all.

Albrighton plays the ringmaster lyrically, welcoming us to the show and directing our attention upward to the tiny figure under the apex pole. Mischievously, he teases us, the audience, that the performer might fall to his death. 'Close your eyes,' he suggests, a triple allusion to Nektar's core theme, to the idea that this is an album best experienced as a trip in the head, and to the crowd itself, childlike in wonder but with eyes screwed shut in fear.

There's a fourth allusion in this song, and it's just as delicious. 'Astral Man' is actually Nektar themselves, offering us this album as something bravely different to what fans expect. It will either make it all the way to the end triumphantly, or it will fall ignominiously 'down to earth.' Either way, Nektar pointedly hope the disc 'has given money's worth.' As it happens, it will repay the purchaser many times over on the following track alone.

'Nelly the Elephant'

Calvert makes his first appearance during the return of the circus effects that close 'Astral Man,' and is on hand here to introduce Nelly and her herd, irrelevantly regaling us with pachyderm facts, including their absolutely true love of oranges – just one more way in which prog widens the mind. Still, let's quibble about whether Nektar's circus would really have an *African* elephant in its troop. Perhaps as a figurehead. I guess Nelly herself is not expected to perform.

This instrumental is by far the silliest track on the album, a second piece of comedy music in a row, but it too is redeemed, this time by a gorgeous melody, a sophisticated arrangement for brass, Albrighton's massive acid-spangled fuzz guitar, and some pre-Larry Fast electronics. Like its predecessor, the track begins with sound effects, including fake elephant calls, before striking up an incongruous tea dance rhythm which suggests Nektar might have had a profitable side business as a light jazz combo. This is soon swerved into the body of the piece, a spectacular club-footed waddle around the ring to the greatest perversion of Nektar's funk you'll ever hear. Step aside Syd Barrett: this is psychedelia's *true* elephant classic.

The title, though – well, that was a problem. Mandy Miller's 1956 single 'Nellie the Elephant', produced by George Martin in his comedy days, was so well known as a children's standard that Nektar surely had the name in mind. The similarity led to some later performers of the Miller song (actually composed by music hall songwriters Ralph Butler and Peter Hart) mistakenly crediting the piece to Nektar, presumably from a lazy copyright search. I know of two cases: Bernard Wrigley's 1976 album *Songs, Stories & Elephants* and the 1984 album *Playmates with Mike and Michelle*. You can almost hear Nelly trumpeting her laughter.

'Early Morning Clown'

From levity, we tumble suddenly to the first of the serious songs that dominate the second halves of each side of the LP. The introduction to 'Early Morning Clown' restates the band's prog credentials with a delicate but ever-shifting succession of changes before settling on a pastoral sound with a bright synth melody, a fine slide guitar solo, and a softly descending chord sequence Albrighton admitted the band cribbed from the 'Würm' section of Yes's 'Starship Trooper'. Albrighton, P. P. Arnold, and Kenneth Cole provide thick washes of harmony, making this portrait of a lonely clown literally cast down to earth in dawn's harsh mirror one of the album's emotional peaks. It's the first song with no intrusion from Calvert.

'That's Life'

The album's longest track (at a mere 6:49) is its bloody, beating heart and its soaring, soulful centre. Arnold and Cole are again on hand to deepen Albrighton's adept vocal – he always seems happiest singing these big, wrenching soul ballads – and wring every last possible drop of passion from its anti-violence message. The band sit behind them perfectly. Moore's gruff bass, which surely should be out of place in something this personal, somehow works well. The track's sudden sprints around the prog block are a fine restatement of the agility of *Remember the Future,* given extra power by the guests' gospel interjections.

There's nothing in the song itself that references the circus theme, but lest we forget him, Calvert is back during an excellent percussive workout in the coda to tell us all the things we can do during the intermission. The first of these suggestions is 'smoke', and it's not just a reference to the no-smoking halls in West Germany, in which the band was used to providing long mid-set breaks so the audience could all rush outside to light their cigarettes.

'Fidgety Queen'

Calvert's back for the last time to introduce the second side of the LP, gaining an unaccompanied feature for the only time on the disc. Given what I said about the old music hall song 'Nellie the Elephant', it's fitting that his introduction to 'Fidgety Queen' is reminiscent of the long-running British TV series *The Good Old Days*, a recreation of music hall, whose compère Leonard Sachs would stoke up the crowd with just the same wild flights of multisyllabic alliteration as Calvert uses, eliciting enthusiastic exclamations and earthy eructations from it.

Like the first side, the song is an opportunity to kick things off with a rocker, knowing that ballads will follow. Its relatively simple high-octane boogie, shouted vocal, and screaming guitar solo made it a live crowd-pleaser – usually the band's encore. For the album, though, the song is punctuated by jazzy sax growls and brass stabs that add real excitement.

Except for one retrofitted line ('she's a circus queen'), the song is another with no link to the album's theme. Its giddy description of an unsuitable but available woman sounds to me like an even slyer version of The Who's already sly enough 'Mary Anne with the Shaky Hand', but I'm surely wrong. Fidgety likely just means she's uncomfortable to be around.

'Oh Willy'

With its fast rock swagger and shrill vocal shadowed precisely by a strident guitar, the bread in this musical sandwich is a direct throwback to ...*Sounds Like This* (and indeed, it was first performed live as part of the 'A Day In The Life Of A Preacher' suite) except of course for the Stax style brass section. The meat is a long, contemplative blues section that ought to do more than simply build back to the rock. It feels like the scaffolding for an unrealised highlight, perhaps a more transcendent guitar solo than the one we get.

Like 'Fidgety Queen', it is clearly an unrelated track conscripted into the concept, and very little, if any, work was done on the lyric to make it fit. It concerns a player in a second-division band whose performance nevertheless energises the singer. Likely there was no way to make Willy – he's a kind of ersatz Jimi Hendrix – a different kind of performer.

'Little Boy'

This acoustic ballad doesn't fit the theme either, but its first line describes the subject as a boy 'covered in make-up', which at least enables the band to spin a tale about him: he's a child in the entourage who longs to perform. It's still not convincing – it could be any child sitting in a dressing room watching their parent get ready and dreaming of doing the same, perhaps even sitting in front of the mirror to pretend after they've been called to the stage. And that one line is all the story we have. The rest of the lyric is sung from the viewpoint of a boy's parents looking fondly down on him and hoping he'll 'never get away' from their love.

Whatever its sentiment, the song is lifted to an anthem by a refrain in which Albrighton is joined for one last time by Arnold and Cole's soulful blend.

'Show Me the Way'

'Little Boy' was a means to shift the listener into a contemplative frame of mind, the priming of the melancholy required so that 'Show Me the Way' can hoist you back skyward. The transition is pure genius: it begins like a revival tent rouser on block chord piano, then the rhythm hardens into deep south boogie with swinging slide guitar and you're fooled into thinking the song's heading in a completely different direction, perhaps to something like Man's 'My Name is Jesus Smith' from *2 Ozs of Plastic with a Hole in the Middle*. But at exactly 0:39, the entire ambience changes to the archetypal frothy Nektar funk. Let it catch you *just right* and the shift is flattening. What follows is one of the band's greatest achievements, a song so joyous it will make you want to abandon yourself in dance, but so emotive you'll be too drained to get up off the floor.

No, there's nothing of the circus here either, simply Albrighton at the height of his power singing like his very sanity depends on making connection with a departing lover. The track's structure is identical to 'Oh Willy'. In the relax, Albrighton duets with Arnold alone (no Cole), his simpler, breathier voice essentially a foil for her free phrasing. You'll wish there were a lot more of this than just one short verse together. They don't really mesh, but you can sense the way she smiles at him across the microphone, and he's in soul heaven. Instead, Albrighton plays a beautifully poised solo through a Leslie speaker, and we head back to a build so chilled it'll stiffen all the hairs on your arms.

'Finale'

Simply a minute and a half of 'Nelly the Elephant' reprised to tie the concept together. It condenses all that song's features into a bitesize recap that fades just when you're bleating out laughter at how ridiculous those humming bass vocals were, all that wild ride of an album ago.

Alternate versions and bonus tracks

Though *Down to Earth* was originally released on quadraphonic, not only has this mix never appeared on CD, but the album has not received the same 5.1 upmix as the band's other period quad tapes. If you want to hear it as if you're in the middle of the circus ring and the band's all around you, you'll have to seek out old vinyl – and something to play it on.

Bacillus released a Europe-only single at the time, consisting of an edit of 'Astral Man' and the full LP version of 'Early Morning Queen'. In North America, Passport Records also released an edit of 'Astral Man' as a single in 1975, but paired it with a slightly edited version of 'Nelly the Elephant' instead. The disc reached 91 on *Billboard*, Nektar's greatest shot at a hit. This pairing was also released in the UK, but as a promo only. I reckon 'Show Me the Way' might also have stood a good chance in the US, but the June 1975 release of Peter Frampton's song of the same name made that impossible. With the European success of 'Astral Man', Bacillus rushed out a second single, comprising an edit of 'Fidgety Queen' and the full LP version of 'Little Boy'. This disc also managed a UK release on United Artists.

For the studio jams recorded during the *Down to Earth* sessions, see *Unidentified Flying Abstract* in the Other Studio Recordings chapter at the end of this book. Oddly, those jams have never been released as an adjunct to *Earth* itself. Indeed, the album has never seen much in the way of reissues, and there has never been a multi-disc or deluxe edition. What latter-day love it *did* receive is consigned to a single expanded CD edition on the Dream Nebula Recordings label in 2005, which adds six 'Original Chipping Norton Mixes' and a short reel of Robert Calvert's vocal session. Purple Pyramid reissued this version of the disc in 2013.

'Astral Man'

There are no sound effects, but the tubas are in place for this mix and are much more prominently featured. Indeed, the weirder sound world makes this arguably a better version, though Albrighton's vocal is a little buried and the track lacks the finished album's shiny top end. It's fun, too, to hear Calvert's thank you in isolation, complete with desultory clapping.

'Nelly the Elephant'

The Chipping Norton Mix, again, has no sound effects and has decided to place Albrighton's guitars hard left and right rather than panning them wildly – but it is every bit as entertaining.

Above: This crop of classic period Nektar posing in a urinal was later used on the front cover of *...Sounds Like Swiss* (2021). From left: Howden, Freeman, Brockett, Moore, Albrighton. *(Beyond Before)*

Right: Nektar celebrated their brief halcyon period in the US with full-page ads such as this one highlighting the 'eight tons of equipment' they toured with. In 1976, the haul included a Mellotron sneaked into the country for Pavlov's Dog. *(Rolling Stone, 5 December 1974)*

Left: First album, *Journey To The Centre Of The Eye* (1971) was a narrative concept about an astronaut who witnesses the end of the world. *(Bacillus)*

Right: Blurring psychedelia into prog to stunning effect, *A Tab In The Ocean* (1972) began Nektar's long association with artist Helmet Wenske. *(Bacillus)*

Left: An eye on the future. Breakthrough album *Remember The Future* (1973) documented a blind boy's triumphant awakening due to his communion with a similarly isolated telepathic alien. *(Bacillus)*

Right: There's still a little space vibe on the cover, but *Down To Earth* (1974) was an attempt to make the band less cosmic. Hence the endearingly silly group shot against a parachute-draped London bus. *(Bacillus)*

Above: *Recycled* (1975) should have been enormous. The band's greatest achievement came packaged in Nektar's most extraordinary sleeve. *(Bacillus)*

Right: Wenske's crayon drawings for *Recycled* were as stunning as the music. This dazzling fold-out image was used on the LP's insert sheet. According to Wenske, the released cover wasn't even the finished artwork. *(Bacillus)*

Left: Roye Albrighton (guitar) and Derek 'Mo' Moore (bass) performing 'Desolation Valley' on *The Old Grey Whistle Test*, 1973.

Right: The band miming to highlights from *Remember The Future* on West German TV in 1974. Roye Albrighton ...

Left: 'Mo' Moore ...

Right: Allan 'Taff' Freeman (keyboards) ...

Left: Ron Howden (drums).

Right: A rare shot of lightshow operator Mick Brockett from the *Remember The Future* broadcast. Brockett would sync the lights to the beat by flickering his fingers in front of the lens.

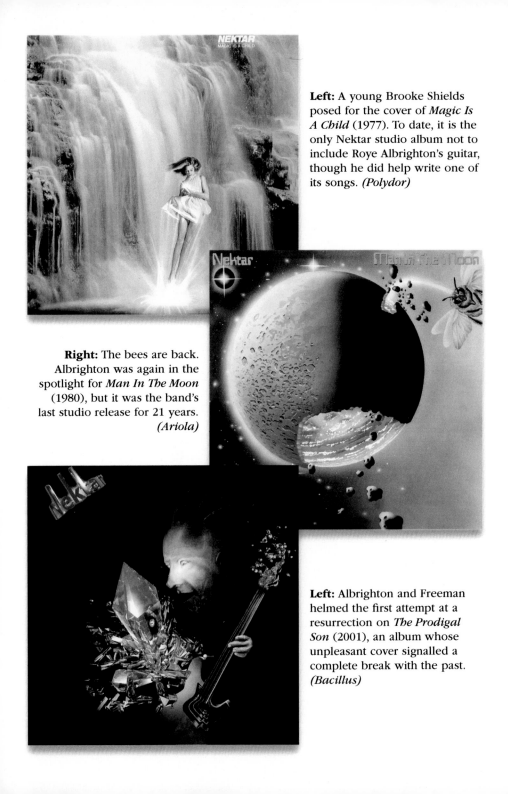

Left: A young Brooke Shields posed for the cover of *Magic Is A Child* (1977). To date, it is the only Nektar studio album not to include Roye Albrighton's guitar, though he did help write one of its songs. *(Polydor)*

Right: The bees are back. Albrighton was again in the spotlight for *Man In The Moon* (1980), but it was the band's last studio release for 21 years. *(Ariola)*

Left: Albrighton and Freeman helmed the first attempt at a resurrection on *The Prodigal Son* (2001), an album whose unpleasant cover signalled a complete break with the past. *(Bacillus)*

Right: Wenske's beeman logo was introduced on *A Tab In The Ocean* and has become the band's trademark. The 'NEKTAR' symbol bottom right is less iconic. Spot the K, win a prize. *(Nektar)*

Above: An awkward release it might be, but Passport Records pushed *Down To Earth* heavily in the US with full-page colour ads like this. *(Rolling Stone, 13 March 1975)*

Right: Though the band complained that they weren't promoted enough in the US, Passport Records did place a series of half-page ads in the press. However, the 'aural ecology' tagline makes the disk sound like hard work. *(Rolling Stone, 6 and 20 May 1976)*

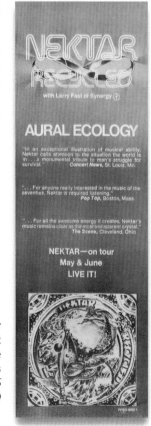

Left: NEARfest brought all four members of the original Nektar together on stage at last in 2002, and it was captured in full for posterity. Here's Albrighton, permed and fighting fit ...

Right: Ex-pat Moore in Patriots Theater on a patriotic bass ...

Left: A rare shot indeed of Freeman working the keys ...

Right: ... and Howden in his nest of drums.

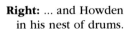

Left: The concert also tempted Larry Fast briefly back to Nektar's synths. Here he is with percussionist Scott Krentz behind. (*All shots from the Live DVD by Classic Rock Productions*)

Right: There was also a commemorative CD of the show, *Greatest Hits Live*. (*Classic Rock Productions*)

Left: The treasure of the 2004/2005 period was the excellent DVD release *Pure* which documented a show in Bonn in March 2005. *(SPV Recordings)*

Right: From the *Pure* DVD, here's Albrighton thrilling the crowd ...

Left: ... and Howden singing the opening to 'A Tab In The Ocean'.

Right: Albrighton, Freeman, and Howden were on board for *Evolution* (2004), an album whose classy Helmet Wenske cover saw Nektar fully embracing their legacy for a new generation. *(Dream Nebula)*

Left: Still weeping after all these years. Though the line-up continued to churn, *Book Of Days* (2008) demonstrated that Nektar were here to stay. *(Bacillus)*

Right: The band's association with Billy Sherwood of Yes led to an album of classic rock tributes *A Spoonful Of Time* (2012). This was the first Nektar studio album with keyboard player Klaus Henatsch. *(Purple Pyramid)*

Left: The *Deluxe Edition* added a karaoke friendly second set consisting of all the same tracks with the vocals stripped off. *(Nektar)*

Right: *Time Machine* (2013). It was the last studio album Albrighton made. *(Purple Pyramid)*

Left: The first studio release by the Howden, Moore, and Brockett incarnation of the band, *The Other Side* (2020), can be seen as a tribute to Roye Albrighton and all the others that Nektar lost across the years. *(Cosmic Cowboy)*

Right: *...Sounds Like This* (1973) was a rough-and-ready double album recorded live in the studio that attempted to file away what was left of Nektar's live set so the band could concentrate on new material. *(Bacillus)*

Left: The original *Sunday Night At London Roundhouse* LP (1974) contained one side of the Roundhouse gig in November 1973 and another of the band live in the studio in March 1974. *(Bacillus)*

Right: The Roundhouse gig was released in full on CD in 2002. The cover merges the original's gatefold image of an eye with a crudely doctored shot of the building, but at least the definite article is finally in place. *(Dream Nebula)*

Left: The matching *Unidentified Flying Abstract* release in 2002 documented the entire March 1974 studio jam. *(Bacillus)*

Right: Albrighton recorded his only solo album, *The Follies of Rupert Treacle* at home in 1998. It received a Nektar release as the bonus disk to a reissue of *Book Of Days* in 2020. *(Purple Pyramid)*

Above: No longer faceless, surely. A promo shot of the 2022 band. From left: Moore, Howden, Brockett, Kendall Scott (keyboards), Ryche Chlanda (guitar), Randy Dembo (bass). *(Nektar)*

Right: A naked fairy smokes a hookah on a mushroom. Okay then. *2004 Tour Live*, Nektar's first major fan club release, was a brightly packaged compilation of performances from 2004 and 2005. *(Treaclehead Productions)*

Left: 2009's cleverly-titled *Fortyfied* live set told promoters that Nektar were back at their peak and fans that they could expect a night out with all the classics. Hidden in the design, a chameleon indicated that the band had changed to match the times. *(Treacle Music)*

Right: The 2021 special edition of *Space Rock Invasion*, which recycled the beeman from *Retrospektive 1969–80*. *(Purple Pyramid)*

Left: The first Nektar compilation (1976) wasn't released in the UK or US. Today it's of note mainly for its simple but striking cover. *(Bacillus)*

Right: The best compilation to date, 2011's *Retrospektive 1969–80*, covers all the highlights from the golden age. *(Cleopatra)*

LIVE ANTHOLOGY 1974-1976

Left: 2019's *Live Anthology 1974–1976* filled five CDs with prime Nektar. The cover painting by Klaus Holitzka was intended for *...Sounds Like This* in 1973, but Bacillus rejected it. Wenske was given one day to paint a replacement. *(Purple Pyramid)*

'Early Morning Clown'
The quite wonderful mix may lack the released version's clarity, but it does pull up Arnold's vocal mike, making her voice much more recognisable. Additionally, we can hear the bluesy variations that Arnold and Cole inject into the verses and their brief scat during the solo.

'That's Life'
Not far enough from the released version to add any revelations, this simply has a less crisp sound that subdues Moore's bass in favour of Howden's unfussy drumming.

'Oh Willy'
For the most part, simply a less-defined mix of the familiar album track, it actually sounds like a slightly degraded tape copy of the master. The central drift is framed in a silence that makes it still more empty, still more a void in the heart of the song.

'Show Me the Way'
Nothing can improve on the perfection of the released track, and equally, no substandard mix could damage it. This version, leaning again on Howden's beat, simply feels like listening to a much-loved song through a fog of tears. There are differences, however: the build is less dramatic, the release less cathartic, and Albrighton isn't duetting with himself in the final verse.

'Robert Calvert Out-Takes'
It's impossible to accurately credit this 2:07 of Calvert's vocal session since it's unclear how much was scripted, and by whom. There's nothing here that sounds like an improvisation, but Calvert may well have decided on his own text and then recited it diligently each time. We hear him chortling his way through three takes of the 'Fidgety Queen' introduction, all word perfect to the final version. Off-mike laughter suggests they're having fun in the control booth, too, and Calvert's certainly enjoying one of his better days.

Recycled (1975)

Personnel:
Roye Albrighton: guitar, lead vocals
Allan 'Taff' Freeman: keyboards, vocals
Ron Howden: drums
Derek 'Mo' Moore: bass, vocals
Additional personnel:
Larry Fast: synthesiser
The English Chorale: vocals (arranged by Christian Kolonovits)
Recorded: July to August 1975 at Studio Hérouville, France and Air Studios,
London, England
Producers: Peter Hauke, Nektar
Released: Bacillus Records LP, October 1975 (West Germany)
Running time: 36:44 (A: 17:38 B: 19:06)

Recycled is an album of superlatives. It contains Nektar's finest music
wrapped in their most extraordinary Helmet Wenske sleeve. It sees the band
at the peak of their musical power, their most audacious and sophisticated
instrumentally, their most focused lyrically, and with a more sumptuous and
beautifully arranged sound than ever before or since. It is the most satisfying
of all their albums and the one with the sharpest and simplest message. The
prog is their proggiest, the funk their funkiest, and even the ballad is the best
they ever wrote. To crown all this, the production is so bright and modern-
sounding that the unwary would listen to it for the first time and swear it
was from a decade later. The rest of prog, which was in decline by 1975, took
years to catch up. And yet it was all but ignored on its release, limped briefly
into the US top 100, did not even manage a British release for 13 months – a
disastrously long time at this point in the 1970s, given what happened in the
interim – and led directly to the band's demise.

It's possible to console ourselves by saying that the album kept good
company. Love's *Forever Changes*, Spirit's *Twelve Dreams of Dr. Sardonicus*,
Van der Graaf Generator's *Pawn Hearts*, and Gene Clark's *No Other* were also
all but ignored on their release and have gained an increasingly rapturous
following since, to the point at which no serious collection is complete
without them. We accept this with prog: some of its finest achievements are
still vastly underappreciated. *Recycled* is the epitome of an album still waiting
for its discovery – and yet here it has been in full view all this time.

Whereas punk saw something new for the British weeklies to fixate upon
in 1977, there was nothing comparable to turn American magazines and FM
radio away on the album's release there in January 1976. Nektar must have
been sure they had created a winner. It was the first album conceived and
recorded after their success, and there's an air of expectant professionalism
about the entire package. It's one that reaches right down to the decision to
record it at France's fabled Château d'Hérouville where Pink Floyd recorded

Obscured by Clouds, David Bowie *Pin Ups*, Elton John *Goodbye Yellow Brick Road* among others, Uriah Heep *Sweet Freedom*, and Jethro Tull attempted to record what became *A Passion Play*. A seriously hip studio for a band with ambitions. The band toured it like rock royalty, flying city to city to perform with a stunning three-screen lightshow in huge venues – and yet it never quite ignited.

The problems were also there from the start and didn't quite stem from the usual ennui and indulgence that overtakes a rock group which suddenly achieves fame after years of striving. There are no infamous stories about Nektar's exploits in America, neither partying, drug taking, or bust-ups onstage. They still seemed as creative as ever. Two songs, 'Marvellous Moses' and 'It's All Over', were already part of the live set, as was a tentative reading of what would become the first side. Just like *Remember the Future* and *Down to Earth*, the band had other fragments ready to fold in. All they needed was to assemble the pieces and come up with the lyrical theme.

But an act that had repeatedly been unlucky with their recording sessions was doubly unlucky here. Hérouville was, just like for Tull, a disaster. Guest Larry Fast, whom the band had encountered at the Passport Records offices in New Jersey, and whose synths would become integral to the album's sound, spent much of his time battling equipment failure. The musicians couldn't even get a worthwhile vocal sound and had to decamp to London to finish the disc at George Martin's Air Studios. This brought them into contact with Martin's engineer Geoff Emerick (*Sgt. Pepper*, *Abbey Road*, *Band on the Run*, and so on), who helped polish the disc but couldn't come up with a mix that passed the band's democratic vote. So Nektar remained in Air for further rounds of overdubs, including a full choir, struggling to make the disc match their vision. A band that had recorded a double album in three days spent over two months fighting this one, and though the album flows with just as light a touch as *Remember,* you can sense the stress between the grooves, in particular that long coda to side one that seems designed to act as a sonic tonic for the nerves.

Though the LP certainly didn't need one, the band decided to give it an overarching theme just like the last two studio releases. *Recycled* was likely meant to return to the grand prog vision of *Remember*, reassuring American fans that *Down to Earth* had merely been an aberration. But the band's message here became uncharacteristically strident. The theme chosen was an admonition over the profligate waste Nektar encountered on their US tours, the wanton piling up of garbage that seemed to be turning the continent into one giant landfill. Albrighton told *Something Else!* in 2012:

It was, for us, a complete eye-opener. After the first week of touring, we were astonished at the throw-away society that the US was accustomed to. It was this shock to the system that decided the route that the new album should take.

We close our ears to the obvious criticism that a jumbo-hopping rock band hardly helped counter all this. Additionally, in these days of campaigns against plastic drinking straws, it's worth remembering that LPs used a huge amount of resources in their manufacture alone. Prog's albums, in particular, likely commanded gatefold cardboard sleeves, probably laminated, to store one or more heavy slabs of vinyl. If your record sold a million copies, that's as much as 140 metric tons of PVC, which purchasers hoarded for a while but then likely disposed of later. Not all these discs ended up in second-hand stores when purchasers moved on or upgraded to CD – if they did, the stores would be floor to ceiling with stacks of unwanted copies of *The Dark Side of the Moon*. The majority were junked.

All that vinyl came from oil. The OPEC embargo from October 1973 to March 1974 played havoc with the supply of the raw material, forcing record companies to meet demand by pressing thinner discs and increasing the percentage of recycled vinyl used in their manufacture – both degraded the sound quality. The measures prompted ex-Bonzo Dog Band member Neil Innes's humorous single 'Re-Cycled Vinyl Blues' in 1974, in which snatches of the songs previously inscribed in the second-hand vinyl keep surfacing, ghosts in the grooves. Nektar's title was likely a reference to all this, though the context is all but forgotten now. The band may even have been making a sly joke about its own propensity to reinvent older pieces as part of a new concept. (It wouldn't be alone: Edgar Winter released an album called *Recycled* in 1977 that made the same inference.)

And on the concept alone, I think the album doesn't succeed. The first side's science fiction vision of a planet made sterile by pollution ought to have been a full-side standalone track just like 'A Tab in the Ocean'. This 'Recycled' suite (and, indeed, this is what is generally meant when the piece is performed live) alone carries the concept just like, say, the equivalent grand statements in albums by ELP.

The rest of the album could have contained completely unrelated songs. There's very little about 'Marvellous Moses' and 'It's All Over' that specifically references pollution and ecological collapse. They predated the concept and were hardly altered to fit better into it. The two new songs, 'São Paulo Sunrise' and 'Costa Del Sol', shift the focus awkwardly from consumerism to tourism, not by itself the worst of our species' transgressions against our environment. The bulk of the latter is merely the inconvenience of other people intruding on one's hideaway. Both seem to bolt on their message.

The odd dichotomy that results is exacerbated by the decision, *Remember*-style, to label the two sides 'Part One' (with seven parts) and 'Part Two' (with four parts) on the original Bacillus release. This convention was followed on its Passport version, though the tracks are here numbered on the labels, confusing the issue. The British release (the band's only disc on Decca) dispensed with the parts altogether and simply listed tracks, as I do here.

Ever since, their status has been uncertain. Either this really is another one-track album – it sure doesn't *feel* like one – or we ought to be able to make a differentiation between pieces that look a lot like sections of a suite ('Cybernetic Consumption', 'Automaton Horrorscope', and so on) and which you'd never play in isolation, and those that are clearly standalone songs which you might. It's the one hiccup in an album which otherwise is close as can be to perfection.

All songs composed by Albrighton, Howden, Freeman, and Moore.

'Recycle'

In total, the first side suite (or 'Part One' of a single album-length track called 'Recycled', if you prefer) runs 17:38, with most of its tracks running just a couple of minutes long. Only the finale 'Unendless Imaginations' is substantial (at 4:36), and that is likely in order to accommodate a lengthy synth coda meant to bolster the rather slim running time. In the following discussion, I accept the section divisions as given, even though they don't correspond to where I would have placed them.

The album certainly begins in dramatic fashion, with a faded-in timpani roll accompanied by the first jet plane whoosh of Fast's synth, before the band slam in with a rhythm that astonishes with its sheer propulsion and which, even more astonishingly, is maintained for much of the suite. Fast remains the feature, playing the overture melody (what I'll call Theme One) on crisp analogue waveforms punched across the stereo field and then laying down a skittering beat in unison with Freeman's stabbing piano chords and Moore's monstrous bass accents. As Albrighton told *Get Ready to Rock* in 2008:

Around this time, we were experimenting with other stuff, and the thought of using choirs and synthesisers were definitely part of it. Synths were starting to grow up at an alarming rate and we wanted to incorporate them in some way. *Recycled* was the perfect vehicle for that.

Above this, Albrighton sings the first two verses and refrain of Theme Two: an anthemic plea for a pause in mankind's headlong rush toward destruction at the hand of our own wasteful culture. Except for huge, crunching chords, Albrighton's own guitar work is restrained to a few metal-anticipating hammer trills and high, despairing squeals.

'Cybernetic Consumption'

A cymbal rush jolts us into this crazed instrumental section in which the band lay down a clanking industrial beat – like a factory turned sentient and lumbering across the virgin landscape spewing smoke and metal shrapnel – to propel Fast's manic synth runs. The whole thing skids across the channels as if rushing back and forth to trample what life remains. It alternates with sections of strident hard rock set to the sound of remorselessly marching feet, reminiscent of Spirogyra's conceptually very similar 1973 classic 'In The Western World', and wild reiterations of Theme One.

'Recycle Countdown'
Identical to the same section of 'Recycle', Albrighton sings two more verses and a refrain of Theme Two.

'Automaton Horrorscope'
An even more schizophrenic instrumental section begins this part, with ash-like cascades of synth accompanying a spoken sermon through a robotic filter. I'm guessing Moore recites this since he's the one who is shown doing it at NEARfest in 2002. It's an emotionless account of the final destruction of our planet, not through war as in *Journey To the Centre of the Eye,* but through our own mismanagement. We're soon swept away – this part is reminiscent of Pussy's comically nightmarish 1969 account of the death of the planet due to our pollution in 'The Open Ground' – leaving only 'recycled energy' to populate our silent world.

It then shifts to the rollicking rhythm of Theme Three, the despairing 'down, down, down' motif that will recur to the end of the piece. Over this, Albrighton splatters angry guitar and engages in extraordinary, scripted duets with Fast while Howden's sticks skitter like an ice-skater frantic to keep on his feet, but it's Freeman's classical piano chords that are the true feature.

'Recycling'
A brief respite for Theme Four, two aching verses and refrains in which Albrighton accuses us directly of our greed – 'you've taken all you need' – and flings back the curtain, ringmaster-like, to reveal exactly what's ahead of us if we don't change our ways. He even seems resigned to the impotence of his message, acknowledging that he's not the first to voice this concern ('songbirds, recycling the same old tune' seems to relate to the bluebird of *Remember the Future,* but definitely references Rachel Carson's 1962 book *Silent Spring* on how pesticides are killing off the natural world) and admitting that it won't do a thing ('still you slave onwards till all is used').

The section ends with comedy of its own: a very silly circus rhythm that troops across the stereo bands as if we're suddenly witness to Nelly and her friends advertising a show of horrors coming to our town. There are potent associations there, but the section, a late addition to the suite, doesn't integrate well. It jolts the listener out of the fury and depression of the rest, kicking the mood somewhere inappropriate with little benefit to show for the interruption – it was always going to be difficult to pull off elegantly. My feeling is that struggling to make sense of this section is the thing that most hamstrings Emerick's mix.

For possible influences, there's Steeleye Span's 1972 album version of hit single 'Gaudete', which shifts slowly toward and away from the listener as if it is a band of carol singers passing in a cloisters. More persuasively, 'The Procession' in Camel's 1974 epic 'The White Rider' presents a homecoming march through cheering crowds and joyously tolling church bells. Both, of course, are triumphal, whereas 'Recycling' is the march of the damned.

'Flight to Reality'

Smashing out of the procession, Camel-like, with another huge timpani roll, this section consists merely of the third and fourth verses and refrains of Theme Three.

'Unendless Imaginations'

Fast's plummeting synth bridges the return of Theme Four with more of those absurdly fast scripted duets before The English Chorale makes its first appearance on the LP, somewhat ludicrously intoning 'do you see? do you see?' first, and then 'going down, going down' over and over like they've just stepped out of The Rolling Stones' session for 'You Can't Always Get What You Want'. It's pompous enough to give prog a bad name.

The suite culminates in big anthemic chords, one last timpani roll, and a crack of doom gong at 2:45. This leaves almost two whole minutes for Fast to play a chiming pattern on the synth – Camel's church bells turned to a requiem – and a synth sequence so achingly similar to Pink Floyd's 'Shine On You Crazy Diamond Part 9', you'll be amazed that Nektar could not have heard it by then, not even in live performance.

'São Paulo Sunrise'

The second side (or, again, 'Part Two' if you prefer) begins with the same synth pattern, slightly slower, to wrongly suggest that the album might be stitched together like *Journey* into one seamless suite. This side runs a healthier 19:07, but there are again sequences of Fast's drift that seem intended to bump up the count. The first song doesn't actually kick-off for 58 seconds and then lasts little over two minutes.

Musically, it begins as pomp rock similar to 'Unendless Imaginations', complete with wordless vocals by the Chorale, but then settles into the second side's dominant rhythm: a funk groove on a steady Howden beat that veers dangerously close to then-emergent disco. This is conceptually appropriate since disco was itself a simplification of Latin rhythms, and it is the hot nightlife of Brazil that is evoked here. Fast tries out the first of his steel drum synth effects, and Howden adds pattering timbales fills.

Though Moore claimed that the song was written in response to Mick Brockett's girlfriend visiting the country and reporting back on the smog that choked the city, the lyric doesn't reflect that theme at all. It merely sets up 'Costa Del Sol' (an entire ocean away) with the wish of a holiday on some 'deserted beach where the air is so free-o' down in bronzy Rio.

'Costa Del Sol'

This moves straight out of 'São Paulo Sunrise' with a bonkers feature for the Chorale, who get to sing about placid seas before Freeman sets up a jazzier funk rhythm on the piano. Albrighton tells us how lovely it is to relax on a virgin island somewhere warm until word spreads. As a result, other people arrive in their droves, turning paradise into a commercialised dive, the pristine sand now unrecognisable under the mounds of 'refuse and waste'. This is apparently the 'cost of the sun' in the title's pun. The Costa del Sol is the coast of Andalusia on the Mediterranean Sea that had then become a popular destination for English tourists on package holidays: grim hotels, bad food, and sunburnt sex. It was as hip to the terminally not so in the 1970s as nearby Ibiza became a decade or so later.

The 'São Paulo Sunrise' theme is reprised, making any division between the two somewhat porous, but the bulk of the song is a gradual build toward 'Marvellous Moses' with some extraordinary synth flourishes by Fast.

'Marvellous Moses'

The first of the two pinnacle songs that form the album's emotional centrepiece is a stately rolling funk to which Albrighton weaves a bizarre story of a superhero who can do amazing feats: fly a boat as if were a kite, raise the height of a mountain armed only with a spoon, and drink down an entire lake. The title suggests Moses is aided in his achievements by divine power, but the song is played dead straight: he's simply a really great guy.

The only sour touch in all this idol worship comes in the final aside 'tourist attraction' that links the song to the two preceding ones but was actually included in early live performances and hence predates them. As far as I can figure out, the idea is that if there were miracles today, we'd simply flock to see them like gawping tourists without attempting to understand their deeper significance. It is the perceived link to the smog of 'São Paulo Sunrise' and the ruined beaches of 'Costa Del Sol' that gives 'Marvellous Moses' any pretence of being part of the ecological theme, though you could well argue that it suggests the gradual draining of magic out of our world so that even our most beautiful natural environments become mere commodities to be exploited like Moses.

Story aside, the song is ridiculously catchy and musically fully assured, both anchored and lifted by Moore's thumping one-note riff and scowling bass flights. Its instrumental middle is a synth-laden masterclass in late prog virtuosity and warm 1970s production.

'It's All Over'

The album's most substantial piece (at 6:17, measured from the previous track's relax into its ballad changes) is this wake for our species, but again we have to be careful of interpretation since the song, lyric largely intact, is older than the theme. It evokes a series of dualities to suggest the inevitability of death – high road versus low road, the latter meaning death in 'The Bonnie Banks O' Loch Lomond', daytime versus darkness – and the madness of our upside-down world.

Building on the wrenching impact of Albrighton's passionate voice, the song uses a synthesiser, of all things, to carry its emotion. This is a breakthrough for Fast himself, but the idea that this coldest of instruments can actually be the most human is an old one, older still than *Wish You Were Here,* which was essentially a manifesto on the subject. Nektar was likely inspired by PFM's 'Impressioni Di Settembre' on *Storia Di Un Minuto* (1972), the first time a synthesiser gained the power to drive a listener to tears and hence effectively rendered all other instruments irrelevant. In earlier Nektar albums, it would have been up to Albrighton's guitar to provoke the clutch in the gut and catharsis in the soul, but *Recycled* eschews guitar solos almost entirely. There isn't one here, just some plaintive picking in an extremely long coda based on Freeman's (again Wright-like) piano and more of that wordless choir.

Alternate versions and bonus tracks

To promote the album in Europe in 1976, Bacillus released a single pairing the 'Flight to Reality' part of the first side suite with an edit of 'It's All Over'. Quadraphonic had waned by 1975, so even if a quad mix was recorded it was never released, and sadly no 5.1 mix has ever surfaced. I've avoided mentioning 8-track cartridges before, but it's worth noting just what a butchery *Recycled* received in the format. To distribute the album over the format's necessary four equal sides, it split the suite in the middle of 'Automaton Horrorscope', and also split both 'São Paulo Sunrise' and 'Marvellous Moses'.

The 2004 CD release on Dream Nebula Recordings consists of the album as released, followed by the entire Geoff Emerick mix. This version has been reissued several times since and is certainly the one to get. Purple Pyramid even released the pair as a double LP in 2012.

The Geoff Emerick mix

There are huge positives to Emerick's mix, which could easily have been the master. We certainly wouldn't question it if this were the version we'd lived with all these years. It's notably leaner, flatter, and not so pompous, with less showy synths and – a point that may make it preferable to many, this writer included – no choir whatsoever. Where the choir will be it is the band that sings or there's simply space for Fast's synth chords or Freeman's piano to ring out instead. The unadorned coda to 'It's All Over' is a real treat.

Emerick emphasises the high percussion, adding a glitteringly attractive surface that helps to add definition to the band's typically congested mid-range. Occasionally you catch surprising hidden touches in the music, such as tubular bells. His 'Cybernetic Consumption' is not so monstrous but has some interesting stereo tricks to play. The procession in 'Recycling' (with a *very* pronounced left-to-right pan, unlike the final version's more nuanced right-to-left) is wince-inducing, but that will always be the case. In 'Marvellous Moses', Emerick handles Moore's playing as melodic counterpoint rather than provider of low throbbing notes, emphasising just how inventive he was as a bassist.

Magic is a Child (1977)

Personnel:
Allan 'Taff' Freeman: keyboards, vocals
Ron Howden: drums, vocals
Derek 'Mo' Moore: bass, vocals
Dave Nelson: guitar, vocals
Additional personnel:
Larry Fast: synthesiser
Julien Barber, Michael Commins, Kermit Moore, Anthony Posk: string quartet
Recorded: March to August 1977 at House Of Music, West Orange, NJ, USA
Producers: Nektar, Jeff Kawalek
Released: Bacillus Records/Polydor LP, September 1977 (West Germany/USA)
Running time: 41:21 (A: 21:32 B: 19:49)

And so this is where it all falls apart. To be fair, the pressures on what was suddenly the older generation of rock stars were enormous in the second half of the 1970s. There hadn't been such a decisive break in popular music since the Beatles swept away almost all the old guard from Britain in 1963 and the US in 1964. Just like then, in came new energy and new ways of engaging with a younger crowd, and it is no consolation at all to know that the punk and new wave artists matured just as the Beatles' and prog's generations had done before them, and so the cycle perpetuated itself. Precious few old bands weathered the change, at least in the short term – Nektar was not one of them.

In reality, as I mentioned in the previous chapter, prog had been declining long before punk's putative year zero. If its high-water mark was the magnum opus albums of 1973, in 1974 the entire scene seemed to convulse as its major artists couldn't decide whether to commercialise like Pink Floyd or react against the excesses of *Tubular Bells*, *Tales from Topographic Oceans*, and *Brain Salad Surgery* by toughening their sound. Many of the major players made more abrasive work in 1974: Genesis's *The Lamb Lies Down on Broadway*, Gentle Giant's *The Power and the Glory*, King Crimson's *Starless and Bible Black*, Yes's *Relayer*. Even the Floyd began to write angrier material that year, though it wasn't released until 1977.

In 1975 many of these players either disbanded, reorganised, reinvented themselves or began the shift toward the middle of the road. That year saw Floyd's requiem for lost dreams, *Wish You Were Here*, Van der Graaf Generator's stripped-down *Godbluff* and *Minstrel in the Gallery*, Jethro Tull's attempt to align themselves back with the heavy rock of *Aqualung*. The year also saw the return of the multi-part pop epic, led by Queen's 'Bohemian Rhapsody', that would soon lead to Manfred Mann's Earth Band's 'Blinded by the Light', John Miles's 'Music', and The Electric Light Orchestra's 'Mr. Blue Sky', as if prog itself had merely been an aberrant road that branched away from 'MacArthur Park' and could now be fenced off as a failed route.

Nektar, too, had reacted to *Dark Side* with an earthier, more commercial album in 1974, but the belated success of *Remember the Future* swerved the band in the opposite direction. I argued earlier that *Recycled* should have come after *Remember*. Instead, *Recycled* is itself the anomaly, a grand prog construct in a year when such things were becoming thin on the ground. In the year of its American release, everyone left around them was shifting ground fast. Nektar's only hope was to shift too, but their future was dealt a near-mortal blow with Albrighton's departure in 1976.

Though it's hard to make a case that Nektar could have enjoyed even greater success in the 1980s, it *was* possible. With hindsight, we can see that *Magic is a Child* was the pivot around which their fortunes now turned, and that *Magic is a Child* failed. There would be no Genesis-style future but a Gentle Giant-esque collapse.

What went wrong? For a start, the circumstances of Nektar's success were now against them. There was no point in staying in West Germany for a band that had already conquered that country and couldn't grow any larger there. As Moore told *The Progressive Aspect* in 2020:

> We basically ran out of places to play in Germany. We were too big to play more than ten gigs throughout the country. We decided that the US was very much like Germany, only better. The fans wanted new music and it had the FM radio stations to support it. Once we came to the US, we had lots of places to play.

So the members packed up everything in late 1975 and emigrated, settling in New Jersey to be close to their audiences on the East Coast and within commuting distance of the Passport Records offices. That soon soured, however, when the failure of *Recycled* prompted the band to ditch Passport for Polydor.

Exactly a year after arrival, Albrighton quit the band to move back to Europe. '[Emigrating to the US] was a big mistake,' he told *The Rocktologist* in 2014. 'We should have stayed living in Germany.'

A split like this likely means one of three things: personal animosity, musical differences, or the wish to forge a more lucrative solo career. We can discount the latter, since Albrighton's star would have burned brighter in America. His own account was one of frustration that the band had done nothing in the studio during that first year in the US. In the 2005 *Magic is a Child* CD booklet, he claims 'there was a period of silence within the band' which left him fired up creatively but with no outlet for new music. This seems implausible since the band had studio time booked for a new album, following which there was another tour scheduled. They had already begun working up new material, including 'Listen', which was included on the new disc and 'Man In The Moon', which was dropped – of course, Albrighton revived it later.

'I had itchy feet,' he explained in the *Retrospektive 1969–1980* booklet, 'and wanted to do something else' – something, in other words, that didn't involve the others. Speaking to *Sea of Tranquility* in 2011, he noted:

> After our *Recycled* tour, I felt my time with Nektar had come to an end. I wanted to move on and do something different – dabble in other styles and just try other things. I guess, in retrospect, we have a choice to take the left or the right fork in the road. I went straight on just to be different and to see what happens. I was still relatively young back then and I wanted to see what the music scene had to offer.

The result was Snowball, a band that flew briefly and then went flump against a wall.

The others told a different story. According to Larry Fast in the *Magic is a Child* CD booklet, 'there had always been differences in outlook and direction between Roye and the rest of the band.' Surely the schism was not as simple as one party wanting to commercialise and the other not. *Magic is a Child* suggested a much more commercial mentality, but so did Snowball's *Defroster* (1978). Nektar needed to streamline their sound if they were to survive in the new atmosphere in the US – *Magic* was the right response.

It's possible that the band's communal, democratic way of working had begun to chafe Albrighton. Every album during his tenure had been jointly credited as 'Nektar'. Every new album afterwards had individual writer's credits. By *The Prodigal Son,* Albrighton had claimed all the music and lyrics as his own. The troubles with the *Recycled* mix also indicate a division in the band. Albrighton had liked the rejected Geoff Emerick mix, as he unloaded on *Retrospektive*:

> The Emerick mix was far superior to the second. It was not my wish to have the second mix released. This was taken out of our hands.

Did he want to be more fully in charge of how Nektar sounded? That at least seems likely, as he continues that the problem wasn't so much that the second *Recycled* mix sounded too American and commercial, but that it simply was 'more other people's idea of what Nektar should sound like.' And as every major rock band knows, as soon as there's success, there are suddenly industry stiffs crowding the studio telling you how you should do your job.

Anyway, he was gone – a decision he also later admitted was a mistake. With the sessions and the tour looming, the others scrambled for a replacement, auditioning 'over 200 guitarists' according to Moore in *Progressive Rock Journal* in 2021 and eventually choosing an unknown American musician called Dave Nelson. At the very least, Nelson did bring a local sensibility to the group, a good calculation for a band hoping to make it back to the charts.

The recording of *Magic is a Child* went relatively smoothly, partly because for the first time since *...Sounds Like This,* the band didn't try to fuse its material into a concept. These were just songs, all relatively short and concise and radio-friendly – an album built for survival in the age of Tom Scholz's Boston, whose first album had stormed the charts in 1976, and Blue Öyster Cult's new slicker sound that had reaped such dividends on *Agents of Fortune*. Rather than hand all the vocals to Nelson, each member shared the microphone. Weird writing credits (the ones on the back cover seem to mention only who penned the lyrics) also suggest a band compromising on their democracy but still determined to work as a team.

Most pointedly, *Magic is a Child* eschewed the prog-style Wenske graphics of the previous releases for simple photographs in the style of other adult-orientated rock albums of the time. The 12-year-old girl with her skirt blowing up on the front and an uncomfortably direct stare on the inner sleeve was a pre-fame Brooke Shields, no stranger to being sexualised like this. She'd already done a nude session for the Playboy publication *Sugar and Spice* in 1975.

It would be wonderful to be able to make a Hollywood production out of the results, a story of redemption featuring hit after hit and countrywide spotlights in heaving stadiums of fawning fans. But there was none of that. There was no hit material, no candidates for saturation radio play. Consequently, there was little Polydor could do to make the disc appealing in the crowded market of 1977. The album stalled at 172 on *Billboard*, the last time ever that Nektar charted in the US. It wasn't even released in the UK.

'Away From Asgard' (Moore, Howden, Freeman, Nelson, Barth)

Cascading Christmas peals of tubular bells and fat slabs of strings kick off this blatant attempt not just to update the band's sound, but to make it irresistible to radio. Its problem is a sonic congestion that was rarely evident in the band's previous music: too many instruments, too many changes for the song's mere 5:30 running length. The listener is faced with sudden harpsichord breaks, dramatic timpani rolls, rollercoaster tonal swoops and peaks, and much more flung at them one after another in a muddled, fussy structure. Even a strong singalong chorus is buried in overproduction. Not just the string section, but Fast's brassy synths joust for the mid-range, making listening a chore rather than the majestic release the band were striving for.

Beneath the froth of the production, however, the band's buoyant tempo and warm chord changes are not so far removed from the second side of *Recycled*. The most notable differences are Nelson's vocal twang and sharper, hotter guitar sound than Albrighton's. The highlight is an audaciously juicy scripted guitar break that erupts into flurries of arpeggios, likely in emulation of Boston's hit 'More Than a Feeling' the previous fall. But compressing all that band's mannerisms into this modest vehicle doesn't quite work. Nor does it help that the song lacks a relatable lyric to anchor it in universal emotions.

'Away From Asgard' is both a celebration of harvest festival in the band's old home in West Germany and an invocation of the Gods of mythological Europe heading off into battle.

'Magic is a Child' (Moore, Howden, Freeman, Nelson, Barth)

The title track, a memory of childhood fairy stories and the mysterious wonder of the world glimpsed outside the bedroom window, is substantially lighter, based on an ornate counterpoint between harpsichord and bass guitar. Under this, Fast's synth sweeps and the string quartet thicken the sound without swamping it. The track is lifted to the album's highlight by a rich harmony vocal that creates a sumptuous, pillowy sound. It's a small pleasure that is here and gone in an instant – just like childhood itself – but counts among the band's best-ever songs.

'Eerie Lackawanna' (Moore, Howden, Freeman, Nelson, Barth)

To get from New Jersey to New York in the mid-1970s, you could ride the Erie Lackawanna Railroad, a line with which Nektar was soon familiar. The ride is celebrated in this, the first of two train songs on the album, but with a slightly altered spelling to evoke the spook of a lonely steam train rolling through the dead of night that seems to leap off the rails and into the void of space, while all the world spins from past to future beneath it. Musically, the song is the band's trademark bubbly funk with conscious roots in the opening section of *Remember the Future*, itself a song about a trip through time.

'Midnite Lite' (Moore, Howden, Freeman, Nelson, Barth)

A second song about Nektar's West German home, this riff-driven hard rock ballad is a far more engaging remembrance of the village of Seeheim than 'Away From Asgard'. It takes us through a description of the cobbled streets and bustling commerce of the community into a dream sequence set in 'forest's deepest dells' beyond. Moore sings strident and effective lead here, winding our thought path through the wooded hills to a magical waterfall over a lake where a 'mystic ship' takes us plunging through the roaring of the water. Its errant (and inconsistent) spelling aside, the title refers to moonlight splashing off the cascades, depicted musically by keening flourishes of Fast's synth.

'Love to Share (Keep Your Worries Behind You)' (Moore, Howden, Freeman, Nelson)

Nektar had done dialogue before: *Remember the Future* included a conversation between bluebird and the blind boy. This rather lovely song about a father's advice to his son, as remembered years later by the now-grown man – Moore sings the father's part, and Howden the son's – is fittingly set to music that references the soundtrack of its generation's youth. It is, specifically, a catalogue of Beatles mannerisms: chiming guitars,

79

slurred, time-dilating vocal harmonies, slurps of backward drums, and pounding piano chords. Its hook is a direct nod to 'She Said She Said', specifically the melody of Lennon's line 'she's making me feel like I've never been born'.

'Train From Nowhere' (Moore, Howden, Freeman, Nelson)

The second side of the LP kicks off with this fittingly muscular tribute to riding trains through the vast reaches of the US, used here as an analogy for the joys of touring in this new frontier. Boston-esque AOR is again the musical springboard, but perversely Nektar choose to interrupt a bright, commercial melody with sour touches that curtail any hope of this becoming a hit. What could have been the archetypal train song, a celebration of the freedom of the rails, becomes what its unhappy title suggests: a hopeful travel through a new land that instead turns to disillusion and defeat.

The song's centrepiece, however, is a marvel: a brief instrumental sequence that begins like a twisted fairground ride but then ramps into prototypical math rock with an excellent guitar solo and Fast's weirdest synth work. It's like opening a window on a different and more extraordinary band of players – I sure wish we'd had an album from *them*.

'Listen' (Moore, Howden, Freeman, Nelson, Albrighton)

The album's longest track is still puny by Nektar standards at just 6:02, and is also anomalous in that it is the one piece of music on the disc that had been started whilst Albrighton was still a member. The band laid down the basic track with him, but after he'd left the others apparently ditched everything except the drum track, which was then slowed to a cavernous thunder. Nothing else remained musically, but Albrighton still gained a writer's credit since the track retained his lyric and, we can assume, at least some of the original melody. The tune and even the phrasing sounds much like him.

It's a superb piece, with very fine reverb guitar work by Nelson over those stately chord changes, his best vocal by far, and an empty room ambience that is strongly reminiscent of the band's early work. For sure, you wish Albrighton was still around to sing and play it, but in the swirls of the track's majestic, bluesy psychedelia, ultimately it doesn't matter – and when that guitar hits you just right, you soar every bit as high as you used to.

'On the Run (The Trucker)' (Moore, Howden, Freeman, Nelson)

While 'Love to Share' comes across as a nostalgic tribute to the Beatles, 'On The Run' brings its influence much closer to home. In the 2005 CD's liner notes, Moore describes it as 'when Pink Floyd meet Foreigner', and he's not joking. The rhythm section is straight out of the former's 'One of These Days'.

Over this, there are the chiming guitars and smooth vocal line (sung by Howden) of AOR rock. Foreigner's first album had been released at exactly the right time (March 1977) to impact it.

The lyric references the Pink Floyd track of the same title, which was about the unstoppable momentum of a busy touring band and its constant fears that the metaphorical plane ride of fame is going to crash. Nektar inverts the feeling to one of elation at being flung skyward by the velocity of fast living, but it's that reckless rhythm that is the litmus test for the track. I love the nod – others may not be so forgiving.

'Spread Your Wings' (Moore, Howden, Freeman, Nelson)

Straight ahead Blue Öyster Cult boogie rock, with dispensable putdown lyrics and a flavour that shifts gears from discordant verses to a jaunty stadium rock chorus, complete with Buck Dharma guitar accents. It's the most commercial proposition on the disc, and in the band's catalogue to date it's the track that strays furthest from the archetypal Nektar sound – the exact same sound, ironically, that Albrighton would pursue on his return. 'Spread Your Wings' formed a fittingly rousing encore for the Nelson incarnation, but it wasn't the way the band would be remembered.

Alternate versions and bonus tracks

No singles seem to have been attempted from *Magic is a Child*. It has received some care on CD, beginning with an expanded 2005 edition on Dream Nebula Recordings. This includes a live version of 'Midnite Lite' from Hofstra University, New York, on 8 October 1977. For more on this concert, see the Live Recordings chapter at the end of this book. It also includes the three bonus tracks detailed below. The 2014 CD release on Purple Pyramid also includes these three bonus tracks but omits 'Midnite Lite' from the first disc. Instead, it devotes an entire second disc to the concert in full.

'Away From Asgard (original demo)' (Moore, Howden, Freeman, Nelson, Barth)

Lacking the extra instruments that so congest the finished version, this demo instead leans heavily on Fast's synths, which give it a purer and more contemporary sound. To its benefit, it also lacks the disjointed building-block feel of the finished work, and the vocals are granted room to breathe. Nelson's guitar orchestra solo is fully in place, and is again the feature. But the bizarre words would always be an impediment to commercial success.

'On the Run (alternate mix)' (Moore, Howden, Freeman, Nelson)

There's nothing to differentiate this from the LP version except a slightly chunkier sound field which I actually find preferable.

'Train From Nowhere (alternate version)' (Moore, Howden, Freeman, Nelson)

Larry Fast's continuing association with the band brought guitarist Robert Fripp into Nektar's circle, however briefly. Fast was then touring with Peter Gabriel, as was Fripp during his long hiatus from band leadership after beheading King Crimson in 1975. Fripp had played guitar on Gabriel's first solo album, released in February 1977, and would soon produce and add guitar to Gabriel's second. He would also soon add scintillating rounds of guitar to David Bowie's hit 'Heroes' and, a little later, play on Blondie's *Parallel Lines*.

With all this forward-thinking, new wave material swirling about Fripp, what was he doing in the studio with Nektar? The session is so embarrassing it doesn't even warrant a mention in Fripp's vast *Exposures* box of the period. Regardless, he plugged in and played keening guitar on 'Train From Nowhere', but the band elected to strip his guitar from the finished track. Hence, even though he gains a pseudonymous credit ('Walt Nektroid') on the album cover, he doesn't actually appear on it. I've always assumed the name was Nektar's sarcastic rejoinder to Fripp's rather starchy character, but Fripp was burying himself behind pseudonyms at the time, in particular performing with Gabriel under the name Dusty Rhodes. Moore claims he invented the name to disguise Fripp for contractual reasons. He might as well have just omitted him from the sleeve.

This track is essentially the same as the finished LP version, except that it includes Fripp's overlay of guitar sound during the instrumental break. In context, Fripp's lemon-sucking sustain is actually appropriate, adding yet another layer of creepy disorientation. It just shifts that already anomalous section even further into the realms of a different, far more adventurous band that we ache to know better.

Man in the Moon (1980)

Personnel:
Roye Albrighton: guitar, lead vocals
Allan 'Taff' Freeman: keyboards
David Prater: drums, vocals
Carmine Rojas: bass, keyboards
Recorded: January to March 1980 at Essex Studios, London, UK ('You're Alone')
and Briar Brook Studios, Bernardsville, NJ, USA (the rest)
Producer: Roye Albrighton
Released: Ariola LP, 1980 (West Germany)
Running time: 40:04 (A: 20:16 B: 19:48)

This album is the only extant document of a period of confusion and churn that followed the band's collapse after *Magic is a Child*. The tour with Dave Nelson had had its moments but, with no chart success, the band lost the last of their chances. An attempt to reconcile with Albrighton in 1978 also failed to reignite but did produce a number of scraps of material Moore would exhume much later for *The Other Side*.

For Albrighton, too, the attempt to move forward had been met with commercial indifference. He quit Snowball after *Defroster*. But there was a new spirit in the air, a generation of slick American-based rock bands that had scored with a sound not so far removed from Nektar's own, and moreover, some of them included British members of earlier, prog-related bands. Richie Blackmore had formed Rainbow with Ronnie James Dio. His old band mate Ian Gillan moved into a jazzier, more sophisticated style on the criminally overlooked *Clear Air Turbulence*. Ian McDonald of King Crimson found himself in Foreigner and Aynsley Dunbar in Journey. The reinvented Anglo-American Fleetwood Mac dominated the charts with *Rumours*. British artists like Al Stewart and Supertramp had also managed to find great success playing FM-friendly rock in America.

On this continent, the emerging AOR that Nektar reacted to on *Magic is a Child* was suddenly the mainstream thanks to Meat Loaf's *Bat Out of Hell* in 1977. Jefferson Starship, REO Speedwagon, Rush, Styx, Toto, and many more had cracked open a vast market in smooth, album-based rock. Even Frank Zappa had found success with a rockier, more mainstream sound.

In England, a rougher form of hard rock infused punk sensibilities into the scene and led to great success for bands like Judas Priest, Thin Lizzy, and UFO, while *Jeff Wayne's Musical Version of The War of The Worlds* (1978) cocked a gazillion selling snook at everything punk itself thought it had achieved. *The Wall* buried an even deeper hatchet in those pretensions the year after. In West Germany, Scorpions had made it big and Eloy looked as if they might follow.

For once, Nektar's snappy name might even have played to their advantage. They could have hoped to be part of this crowd.

Certainly, the plan was not to return to the prog style of *Remember the Future*. Albrighton brought Freeman on board in 1979, added a new drummer and bassist, and pieced together a comeback album: *Man in the Moon*, expressly designed to make space for Nektar in the market – and what a pointedly on-the-zeitgeist LP it was! The back cover photo shows a band of archetypal FM rockers, all shiny mullets without a trace of facial hair, looking sharp as tacks in their big rock'n'roll business suits. Albrighton, clearly the leader, clenches the neck of his guitar tightly with both hands, likely signifying his hold on the band. The front cover painting wasn't wonderful, but it did look of a piece with Boston and Rainbow. There was even a new Nektar logo: a bee's head whose Sony Walkman-style earphone lead spells out the band's name.

A more cynical commentator would conclude the band had calculated every part of their image and that the music itself needed only be competent enough to get airplay to springboard it into what was expected – and indeed, proved to be – a whole new decade of astonishing success for men with big hair.

But the album was hobbled from the start. Despite being recorded in the US, it was never released there. It limped out only in West Germany, Italy, and Greece on the German Ariola label. Lead track 'Too Young to Die' was flung out as a single to no avail. Perhaps the band might have settled back in the country and rebuilt their base, but Freeman didn't want to do that. Nektar struggled on for two years before Albrighton finally pulled the plug.

Man in the Moon shares more than just its hungry commercial sound with *Magic is a Child*. Like its predecessor, the writing credits are strange. Some tracks list 'Nektar' separately from other contributors. For example, 'Too Young to Die' is credited to Nektar, Albrighton, Freeman. In cases like this, I assume by 'Nektar' the four members of the band are meant and simply list everyone in alphabetical order. But other tracks do list the members individually *as well as* other writers. For example, 'Telephone' is credited to Albrighton, Rojas, Freeman, Albrighton, Freeman.

It's hard to parse the intention here (though there *was* a convention in West Germany to list lyricists separately from tunesmiths, even if they were the same people) and so again, I simply list the given band members alphabetically.

'Too Young to Die' (Albrighton, Freeman, Prater, Rojas)

The style is fully formed from this lead track: brightly focused vocals, brooding electric guitars, steady bass pulse, pin-sharp technical drumming, all carrying a mid-tempo, minor key rock anthem with a soaring ultra-commercial chorus in which the singer laments an instantly relatable subject: the break-up of his relationship. What excitement there is comes from a fine instrument-by-instrument build in the last third of the song – but the piece is FM fluff, and frankly, it could have been anybody.

'Angel' (Albrighton, Freeman, Prater, Rojas)

Albrighton's voice has glimpses of its old, soulful power on this widescreen power ballad that leans heavily on Freeman's sumptuous church organ. It's another break-up song, with a succinct running time (3:30) that suggests radio play in mind.

'Telephone' (Albrighton, Freeman, Rojas)

A second, similar ballad in a row, and again at radio length. This one is slightly more positive lyrically: the singer wonders whether to call his partner in the dead of night. Though they're apart, they are spiritually together, bonded by love. 'Telephone' is an attractive song, sung extremely well and bedded on Freeman's adept electric piano and some then-fashionable bass slurs by Rojas.

'Far Away' (Albrighton)

We dearly needed a rocker after the two ballads, but here's another gloomy three minutes of existential angst: distance, here, is doubt. The singer is again separated from his lover, but now he seems ambivalent on whether he cares about her or is about to revel in the freedom of striking out on his own.

'Torraine' (Albrighton, Freeman, Prater, Rojas)

There are only two tracks on *Man in the Moon* that crack the five-minute barrier. This first side closer (the shorter at 5:25) begins as another electric piano ballad, erupts briefly into a soaring, heartfelt cry of love for the woman of the title, and then satisfyingly shifts gears to whirling touches of proggy AOR with flittering synth and succulent Boston guitars that would have sounded right at home on *Magic is a Child*. It then climbs further still towards an anthemic finish in which a stricken Albrighton keens the name over and over in the desolate ecstasy of his need.

'Can't Stop You Now' (Albrighton, Freeman, Prater, Rojas)

Bouncy pop opens side two with a by-the-numbers AOR chorus and all the right gear shifts. For all its calculation, it never quite ignites, lacking that irresistible catchiness that would put it in a million teenage bedrooms.

'We' (Albrighton, Freeman, Prater, Rojas)

This is an incongruously upbeat paean to a woman who kicked the singer out the door – he's in the hall begging to be let back in. The problem here is not just that it sounds like 'Can't Stop You Now', but that it includes exactly the same baritone background vocals, making it an awkward piece of sequencing. Previously synth-adverse Freeman gets to make delighted noises on the instrument and there's a muscular guitar solo, but the vehicle's simply not good enough for casual listeners to stay switched on long enough to hear them.

'You're Alone' (Albrighton)

Although this one begins as a very welcome 'It's All Over' style ballad on acoustic guitar, shadowed by subliminal synths and sensitive touches of piano, it inevitably blasts out power chords as if Albrighton wants to project the rage of his loneliness to a whole arena of similarly afflicted individuals. We're all looking to connect, he claims, all trapped in our emotional blindness. It's a welcome reversion to the band's classic style from a man that, it seems to me, chose to turn off his commercial pressures for just one moment, and be himself.

'Man in the Moon' (Albrighton, Freeman)

This masterwork is the album's longest track by far at 6:42 and the one most attuned to the classics of old – it even kicks off with a bass whoosh similar to that which opens *Remember the Future*. It's another of the band's dialogue songs, this time a conversation between Earth and Moon as they wish each other well in their lonely circling through space.

There's a Pink Floyd link here: the song evokes the poem 'Two Planets' by Allama Sir Mohammed Iqbal, whose first verse was lifted, almost verbatim, by Roger Waters for the original opening to the track 'Echoes'. A dramatically driving minor key epic, it's at a stately Floydian tempo and contains synth and guitar solos achingly similar to those of 'Shine on You Crazy Diamond', so the connection is not as fanciful as it sounds.

However, there's one potential hiccup that excited new listeners have to navigate. The moon's voice uses a bizarre vocal treatment, the same octave-dropping device Frank Zappa employed on 'I'm The Slime', to make it sound solemn and soulful, though here it comes across as slightly comical and a little racially suspect.

Alternate versions and bonus tracks

Ariola released a single in West Germany to promote the album, comprising the two side starters 'Too Young to Die' and 'Can't Stop You Now'. It took until 2002 for *Man in the Moon* to warrant its first and only CD release – on Voiceprint in the UK. Two bonus tracks from the sessions were appended as follows. These tracks were listed as if they were part of the album itself, regardless that the first is plainly a repeat of the opening song. That was it for the album on the format, save a couple of Japanese issues and a curious two-disc release on Cleopatra in 2012 that combined the full Voiceprint CD with *Evolution* and the *Always* EP (which included rerecordings of two *Man in the Moon* songs). See the *Evolution* chapter for more.

'Impossible Years (Too Young to Die)' (Albrighton, Freeman, Prater, Rojas)

A carbon copy of 'Too Young to Die' running the same length and with no significant difference that I can discern.

'Straight Jacket' (Albrighton)

Faster and crazier than anything on the album itself, this is simply high-octane B-side pop with a throwaway chorus, though some tricky changes in the instrumental break and a scribbly final guitar solo add fleeting interest.

The Prodigal Son (2001)

Personnel:
Roye Albrighton: guitar, bass, vocals
Allan 'Taff' Freeman: keyboards
Ray Hardwick: drums
Recorded: Rich Bitch Studios, Birmingham, England (date unknown)
Producer: Roye Albrighton
Released: Bacillus Records CD, September 2001 (Germany)
Running time: 53:45

There's no credit confusion about the band's comeback album. Everything is credited solely to Albrighton, who led Nektar's second resurrection far more fully than even the *Man in the Moon* incarnation.

Freeman was back on board, but there was no separate bassist this time, and no need of one for a band that as yet declined promotional work. Certainly, Albrighton had learned the craft of the lone record producer, having put together an album all by himself in his home studio in 1998 – see *The Follies of Rupert Treacle* in the Other Studio Recordings chapter at the end of this book for more. Freeman and one-time-only drummer Ray Hardwick gave the disc some legitimacy as a band release, but essentially they were used only to handle the parts that Albrighton could not do by himself, and the synth facsimiles of keyboards and drums on *Follies* suggest maybe he could have.

In interviews, Albrighton claimed it as a personal work. For example, to *Aural Innovations* in 2011, he explained:

[My doctor] said I've had hepatitis since the age of 16 that's been eating away at my liver and it's in its last stages. You can imagine my shock. I asked if he could give me any medication for it and he said, no, we're talking transplant. It was that far gone. So I had to wait until a donor became available and then have it done. And unfortunately, I'm one of those people who don't recover very quickly. This is what *The Prodigal Son* songs came out of. It was my experience of being in the hospital in that period. [...] What kicked me around and what caused the worry as to whether I'd recover or not was the drugs they gave me. But I finally came out of it, everything's okay.

He told *Something Else!* in 2012:

While I was laying there recuperating, I thought to myself that regardless of how long I have to live after this illness, I would spend it with my old band and make some more music.

In the booklet of *The Prodigal Son,* he thanks everyone for 'giving me a second shot at life.'

Though *The Prodigal Son* was the best thing to bear Nektar's name since *Recycled* – which is not actually intended as any kind of comparison with that work – it was largely ignored on release and has received scant attention ever since. The abominable cover, which matches the band with the chill-out dub scene of prog-related bands such as The Orb, FSOL, and Steve Hillage's System 7, probably doesn't help the unconvinced tentatively lifting this thing from a record store rack. It was released on CD only, in Germany on Bacillus and the US on the tiny, Philadelphia-based Dead Ringer label, and has, to my knowledge, never had any kind of reissue except once in a mini-LP sleeve (even though it was never an LP!) in Japan in 2014. There are no alternate versions, bonus tracks, or singles.

All songs composed by Albrighton.

'Terminus'

This and 'Oh My' are listed together, forming Nektar's longest track on this album (at 9:09) and its most substantial piece of uninterrupted music since the *Recycled* suite. It's unclear exactly where the break is. I assume here it's where the rhythm picks up at 4:37, but a repeat of a 'Terminus' choral motif at the end of 'Oh My' probably means the pair were always intended as another suite.

First, we catch a cosmic radio tuning beyond the music of the spheres to discover a snippet of *Remember the Future* floating through space like the broadcasts in the 1997 movie *Contact*. After 46 seconds, this leads straight into dignified slow rock with laser-bright guitar that reveals a band still only just emerging from the AOR of *Man in the Moon,* as if that album had been released last month rather than 21 years ago. There's certainly little discernible wear of time on Albrighton's voice, which he bathes in sumptuous layers of harmony. At 4:06, the track drops off suddenly into an ambient bridge section in which – beginning the religious references that saturate the disc – Albrighton's one-man choir intones 'heaven...freedom...always...always' twice before the 'Oh My' rhythm kicks in.

'Oh My'

Jumpy funk flings the band suddenly forward to contemporary prog stylings. Albrighton relates his redemption from the midnight doubts of 'Terminus' to this heavenly 'land of dreams' highlighted, a little blatantly, by a searing guitar riff extrapolated straight out of Andrew Lloyd Webber's chorus to 'Jesus Christ Superstar'. Over the fade, the 'heaven...freedom...' choir returns, this time with a gospel swagger.

'Now'

Albrighton's first ballad of the disc is an effective and highly affecting hymn in praise of his redemption from near death. Accompanied at first only by gentle electric guitar, he explains the precarious nature of our lives, teetering forever on the verge of disaster, and how he himself encountered a bluebird-style angel who saved him from his troubles. Now he wants to extend the same gift to us. By the third verse, Freeman has added subtle runs of twangy, harpsichord-like piano. A minute and a half in, the drums propel the song into the same kind of growly triumphal rock as in *Man in the Moon*. The surprising inversion of a brief acoustic instrumental gives us a moment's pause to reflect, before Albrighton's adept guitar solo lifts us back skyward.

'I Can't Help You'
A fine mid-tempo AOR rock track that would again have been right at home on the previous album. Albrighton recounts his physical and emotional travails but refuses to offer us succour in our own.

'The Drinking Mans Wine'
That's not a typo, simply one of Nektar's recurrent strangely punctuated titles. It's the second power ballad, with a trajectory identical to the first: an introductory verse accompanied only by guitar before the band slams in. Albrighton sings of his yearning for his lover, comfort in the turbulence of his days, to a skirt-swaying, 3/4 rhythm that climbs to a complex, attractive chorus.

'Shangri-La'
Big, stadium-filling anthemic rock with searing power chords that frame a sensitive lyric about the paradise hidden inside all of us. A little awkwardly, it is the second song in a row in 3/4, but it does give the impression of thousands of people slowly waving light sticks over their heads. Albrighton repeats the *Man in the Moon* trick of shadowing the fade chorus with baritone harmonies.

'Salt and Vinegar and Rhythm and Blues'
As the title suggests, this is gritty, high-octane rock'n'roll. Albrighton's crunchy guitar riff and soulful bleating push the track through its changes, spinning a tale of a guy happy to get his kicks in the working man's everyday world rather than coast on the fantasies of fame. Freeman provides an understated organ solo, but it is Albrighton's piercing guitar solo that makes the song more than just a local band playing off down the end of the bar. It ends with a great bass guitar workout before an organ flourish and a staged collapse.

'The Prodigal Son'
A sampler of contrasting AOR textures, the track veers abruptly from a swinging rock introduction with vicious chainsaw guitar, to a languid body of brooding verses based on an insistent one-note bass riff that occupies the entire rest of the song without the longed-for shift back to the rock of the

opening. The point is to signal contentment after turmoil in the hope it will never return. Instead, it flitters softly away to leave only the hymnal tones of more of those baritone harmonies: peace at the end.

Lyrically, Albrighton acknowledges the changes he's been through, as have we all – 'Lord knows how we survived' – and claims to have come out the other side wiser and humbler, returning to us like the son in the Bible story looking for our acceptance rather than our scorn.

'Be Tonight'

Simple celebratory pop in which Albrighton's singer contrasts his own lucky life and loving wife with a crazier associate John, wishing, just a little, that he was still out there running in the mouth of the night.

'Day 9'

In contrast to all those fat, uplifting songs in major keys, it's satisfying to end the album on this more complex and episodic coda. It begins by briefly reprising 'The Drinking Mans Wine', slips into a floating section flavoured with the same wildlife sounds as on *The Follies of Rupert Treacle*, then bursts into chunky rock with beseeching choral vocals and a scribbly slop of guitar that sounds like Albrighton trying out ideas for several solos one after the other. Radio interference drags this gradually back into the tinny transistors that began the album. We switch channels away just as Freeman is trying out the makings of an organ accompaniment, and drift serenely onward through the droning depths of space.

Evolution (2004)

Personnel:
Roye Albrighton: guitar, lead vocals
Randy Dembo: bass, vocals
Allan 'Taff' Freeman: keyboards, vocals
Ron Howden: drums, vocals
Recorded: June 2004 at The Chapel Studios, South Thoresby, England (basic tracks), and July 2004 at Delta Recording Studios, Chartham, England (overdubs)
Producer: Julian Gordon-Hastings
Released: Dream Nebula Recordings CD, October 2004 (Europe)
Running time: 1:01:30

After the original band's triumphant return to live work at NEARfest in June 2002 (see the Live Recordings chapter at the end of this book for more), most of the members remained for this reinvigorated studio album. Only Moore dropped out following shows in 2003. He was replaced by bassist Randy Dembo, the first of what turned out to be a revolving door on the instrument. Up until Albrighton's death, there were no two studio albums with the same bassist, though Dembo was back as a member of the reformed 2018 band playing in a two-bass configuration with Moore. This was also Freeman's final album as a member of the band, after which he left the music business altogether.

We're lucky to have the disc. With little interest from mainstream labels – prog's resurrection was still in its infancy in 2004 – the band decided to release the album on their own Dream Nebula Recordings imprint, on CD only, financed by fan donations. Every supporter's name was listed in the booklet. It came wrapped, at last, in a new Helmet Wenske painting, signalling the band's return to its full power. Prog watchers will also be delighted that Albrighton passed over production duties to the son of Caravan's leader Pye Hastings.

With the return of the old band came a return to at least part of the original Nektar ethos. The three-minute pop songs were shelved in favour of an album of longer, more involved tracks, only one of which is under six minutes. Radio play was never expected nor intended to be the means by which the work built a commercial following. But not all of the ethos could be retained. On its release, Albrighton noted to *Progressive Ears* that physical distance – he was the only member who lived in Europe, the rest were all in New Jersey – caused him to be largely a leader in absentia and so the band's old way of working communally had been abandoned:

Because of the pressures of us being so far apart, I tend to come up with most of the song now, and take that with me [to the others], and then we'll sit down with the song and decide what we're going to do with it and dissect it right there and then, as opposed to building on it.

The disconnect even extended to rehearsals for live work:

It's not a perfect setup, but all the boys over there, they know every song inside out, so what they do is rehearse as a three-piece over there, and I rehearse on my own over here, with concert tapes, until it's time to do the tour. Then I fly over there, or they fly here, depending on where the tour starts, and we rehearse for two days, and we go out on the road.

Evolution was extremely well received by the band's existing fans. It has remained a Nektar favourite: if not a full return to their golden age glories, then a pleasing acknowledgement that the band had finally accepted their past while deepening and maturing with age.

Is it a concept album? There are lines of continuity that link many of the songs. For example, 'After the Fall' refers to Earth as 'the mother of all', tracing a line back to an earlier song, 'Old Mother Earth'. Though the last three songs on the disc certainly do belong together, I'd hesitate to claim that *Evolution* is conceptual overall. Its recurring theme of the world careening toward destruction is familiar enough from *Journey to the Centre of the Eye* and *Recycled* that we can see it simply as another instalment in a Nektar preoccupation in the same way that, say, madness was a Pink Floyd preoccupation. At best, *Evolution* is merely an update of the same warnings Nektar were giving us three decades ago. I wish, a further two decades on, that I could say they made any difference.

All songs composed by Albrighton except where marked.

'Camouflage to White'

Take *another* trip back in time. Here we are floating in space again, channelling the detritus of the years: NASA radio conversations, far-off children's laughter, disconnected instruments and voices merging into fragmentary symphonies. All of a sudden, the band crashes into muscular, King Crimson-style math rock, overlaid with plumped-up guitar chords like the pillowy dazzle of sudden sunbursts, and Albrighton lets off the firecrackers of a solo. It all stops short as if stunned, leaving us back in those weightless tumbles of synth sweeps and shuttle-to-control broadcasts.

Howden's assured drum break flips this aside for Nektar funk, a band throwing jerky shapes across the cosmos. 'Out here the stars are still shining,' Albrighton sings, 'recalling past events.' And it's not just the golden age that is evoked. As if to demonstrate continuity of purpose, those *Man in the Moon* baritone harmonies are back, too.

But old Nektar means old fears. The song warns against unprecedented dangers and threats against which the only shelter, according to the title, is in surrender. Certainly, there's nowhere to hide when the bombs start falling from space as they do so viscerally in the song's next leap into orbit.

'Old Mother Earth' (Albrighton, Freeman)

A piano ballad begins this track, in which Albrighton at his smooth, smoky best declares his devotion both to his life partner and to the planet itself. The romance is heartfelt and achingly personal, and the song's conceit – a lesser beauty equated to a greater beauty – potent and clever, though, of course, both subjects would likely object to the adjective in the title. The care, delicacy, and C major simplicity of this section are new for Nektar, revealing songwriting strength for both writers that even 'It's All Over' didn't suggest.

But this *is* Nektar, after all, and a minute in, the band erupt and the message darkens. Against a sinewy funk rhythm, Albrighton rails at the destruction of the natural world to fuel the greed of the rich. The big chorus is a call and response cry for them to change their ways while there's still all this splendour to save, and for us to make a stand for freedom.

At 3:15, the track shapeshifts again, becoming a plaintive electric guitar piece over softly keening synth and softly floating drones. It's the most delicate moment in the band's career to date, a perfectly poised, scripted melody that hangs molten as dawn sunbeams caught in the last fragments of dew. The rhythm darkens and Albrighton switches to acoustic guitar to reiterate the same theme, broadening the vista like the cold light seeping over vast forested valleys. This *is* worth saving, Albrighton seems to be saying. It's certainly something we cannot afford to lose.

At 5:18, power chords and brief seagull-like flecks of guitar blast us into the full force of Albrighton's guitar playing and the triumphal return of the chorus, crowning one of the band's best latter-day achievements. In the song's last minute, we return to Freeman's piano piece, this time totally unaccompanied – a welcome nod to the musician that so rarely stepped into the spotlight.

'Child of Mine'

Swirls of synth merge into piano, slide guitar, and acoustic guitar for a languorous call to a newborn child to wake up and see his father for the first time. There are no tricky tempo or volume changes here, no restless prog inversions, just the slowly moving chords and Albrighton's perfectly pitched voice summoning a new consciousness to life in the shelter of his arms. The true treasure, however, is again Freeman's piano playing, which hovers fragile accents over the top.

'Phazed by the Storm'

The first of the album's epics (at 9:24) opens with big screen rock statement written all over it, from the leisurely tempo and demonstrative minor key chord changes, to the bright guitar that climbs to peals of bell-like sounds over. Albrighton's voice is a golden age declamation in the midst of the drama, a voice shouted from windblown cliffs.

But this, in truly epic fashion, also shifts. At 2:31, a final crashing organ chord decays into spritely electric guitar arpeggios that flicker much like Robert Fripp's guitar did in the 1980s. A new song builds on this foundation, contrasting Dembo's rock-solid bass with Freeman's sweet, celeste-like synth notes. To this, Albrighton weaves a story of divine help in the midst of loss and uncertainty in soft verses and vast, rock anthem choruses. The storm is a prison of earthly cares, he tells us. God creates release into paradise where we are 'free to wonder, and taste the fruit of life's tree.'

At 5:26, we change again to stately funk, over which Albrighton plays a carefully scripted solo, followed by more Fripp-like arpeggios at 6:59, to which Dembo adds a surging rock bass line. Abruptly, Albrighton leads off with another of those baritone vocals, this time in a funky rap style, which either adds an unexpected new flavour to the Nektar mix or squashes the track flat, depending on how you feel about such things. Close your eyes and this could almost be a dance track, again evoking shades of Fripp, this time of his discotronics. You're still wondering whether to dare yourself to your feet when the track fades away, saving yourself the prog fan's eternal dilemma of whether music is meant to move more than just the toes.

'Always'

A near classic, this excellent hard rock ballad begins with a brief aberration of unaccompanied vocal scat (which recurs again in the middle and end of the song) before the band blasts in with its patent slow funk and Albrighton's scalding fuzz guitar riff. This soon switches to acoustic guitar and a lament about our uncertainty in the face of big decisions. Why must our bad choices last forever, Albrighton wants to know, separating us from each other for all time: 'If there's a heaven, why can't it be there inside you?' The track's thunderous heart is Howden's sudden drum fill at 4:11, rousing Albrighton to perform a lustral solo.

'Dancin' Into the Void'

Imagine a smoother, groovier version of Family's 'See Through Windows' played with Nektar's spry beat like a cat on a griddle and with a vocal that is not so much crooned as whispered straight in your ear. It's actually even more alluring than that sounds, a pool of delicious sound into which the listener is slowly lowered so that all their senses tingle with pleasure.

Now contrast all this with the lyric, which concerns the way our species has taken all that was good about the world and perverted it into violence, commercialism, and pollution. The album title is a reference to Albrighton's claim that 'there's no solution' to all these problems, 'just evolution.'

The track's centrepiece is another of those moments that is going to polarise old fans trying to assimilate the reformed band. The rhythm drops away to a gliding jazz break with a brief pure-toned guitar solo. Then Albrighton comes in even closer to your ear. 'Let's just draw a picture,' he murmurs, 'of this world we all live in.' Not singing, talking, and with all the soft, sensual persuasion of a soul singer's mid-song seduction routine.

But again, the more appealing the sound, the more apposite the lyric. Albrighton invites us to imagine aliens visiting Earth and witnessing all we're doing to ourselves and the planet – oh, let's say, the aliens from *Journey to the Centre of the Eye*. 'Let's face it,' Albrighton sighs, 'it's a hopeless task. We haven't got a chance.' We couldn't even save it now if we tried, given the inadequacy of our own abilities to make meaningful reform: 'How do you fix a rainforest?' Albrighton wonders, 'or mend holes in the sky?' And heading off into space won't help, either, not when we need 'a million arks' to save everyone and the nearest habitable planet is 'a million years away'.

The track ends with a bubbly coda and a singalong refrain that yearns for us to feel wonderful in our disgrace – never was planetary destruction so captivating.

'The Debate'

All right, so 'Dancin' Into the Void' left you conflicted over its awkward mix of positive music and negative words. Here's where things get *really* complicated. That was merely the first of a trio of songs on the same subject, and 'The Debate' is just as contrary.

Albrighton has no salve to offer. The void we're all reeling merrily towards is even more agape. He lays it out for us: a barren, radioactive landscape of 'darkness, dust, and pain.' We can't do anything to avoid it since we're in constant conflict with each other. So let's talk it over. Failing that, those 'million arks' seem like a mighty fine fallback. Albrighton even envisions building the ships and setting off into space: 'it's time to go searching again.'

While you're cataloguing all the conceptual continuity, take a moment to recognise just how *weird* the track is. It begins as a fast-paced 1980s style rocker – you can imagine the singer clapping along with his shirt sleeves folded back – but the chorus is a crazed barrage of overdriven synth runs like a sped-up Soviet anthem punctuated by Albrighton's shouted exhortation 'debate!' Then there's a swooning AOR middle section with those baritone harmonies, a sequence of vast, booming metal chords over which a slide guitar squeals like plunging missiles, and a manic math rock workout with tight ensemble work and Albrighton's heaviest and most substantial solo of the album. By the time it fades, you're thoroughly exhausted and you've forgotten what the argument was supposed to be about.

'After the Fall'

And then there's *this*: a relatively brief requiem opening with the familiar mix of adeptly played acoustic guitar and Freeman's sensitive piano touches. It's another 'It's All Over' set in the ruins that the previous track left in its wake, the survivors picking themselves up to reflect on all that went wrong. Between verses, Freeman carries the lament with great sensitivity and restraint. Fittingly, what might have been an emotionally purgative Gilmour-style solo at the end is curtailed in mid-flow, frustrating the listener. Instead, we get the nightmare return of the opener's orbital freefall – space turned bleak indeed.

Alternate versions and bonus tracks

Great as it was, *Evolution* has never garnered expanded editions or even much in the way of reissues. It has come out only twice since its original release: in Germany in 2008 and Japan in 2014. However, the band did release a follow-up CD EP called *Always* in 2005 comprising edits of 'Always' and 'Child of Mine' and two 'live in the studio' versions of tracks from *Man in the Moon*. These are new recordings from the *Evolution* sessions in Chapel Studios, purpose unknown. In a more just world, they would have brought the band notice and acclaim, but as usual, no one was listening.

The *Always* EP has been incorporated twice into other releases: a two-disc set on Cleopatra in 2012 that combined *Man in the Moon* with *Evolution*, and the 2014 Japanese CD.

'Telephone (live in the studio)' (Albrighton, Freeman, Rojas)

Slower and dreamier than the original, this new version wafts in on subtle layers of electric piano and acoustic guitar and is hushed by washes of cymbals to form an uneasy lullaby. Albrighton sings with feeling, accented by Howden's tasteful drum fills – it's an aching triumph.

'Angel (live in the studio)' (Albrighton, Freeman, Prater, Rojas)

Also bedded on subtly reverbed acoustic guitar and Freeman's understated electric piano flourishes, the new 'Angel' is a less strident power ballad than the original and more nuanced in its heartbreak. Albrighton rides the depths of his passion, alternating breathless, uncertain phrases with soulful scat that strains to lift the piece out of its self-imposed confines.

Book of Days (2008)

Personnel:
Steve Adams: guitar, vocals
Roye Albrighton: guitar, lead vocals
Desha Dunnahoe: bass, vocals
Ron Howden: drums, vocals
Steve Mattern: keyboards
Recorded: 2007/8 (location unknown)
Producers: Roye Albrighton
Released: Bacillus Records CD, May 2008 (Germany)
Running time: 54:33

Churn continued to plague the band, due at least in part to clashes between members and Nektar's ongoing difficulties in gaining commercial headway. The group was by no means a full-time proposition. Management issues also stalled them. Albrighton even went back to performing solo for a while.

Though *Book of Days* was recorded in 2007 by the line-up given above, by the time of its release a year later, Nektar had convulsed yet again, and now consisted of Albrighton, Howden, bassist Peter Pichl, and keyboard player Klaus Henatsch. To avoid confusing fans, the CD booklet listed only this new line-up and did not mention recording details at all. In fact, information remains sketchy for *Book of Days*. Even on the band's own website, which relegates the disc to one of its 'also rans' (alongside *The Prodigal Son*, *A Spoonful of Time*, and *Time Machine*), the only players listed are Albrighton and Howden. For all that, this was the first studio album since *Man on the Moon* to gain release on LP, though it had to wait until the vinyl upsurge in 2019 to achieve it.

With all this happening, the album itself was never actually completed. Albrighton claimed to *It's Psychedelic Baby* in 2012 that the band ran out of funds and so could not finish work on it:

It was supposed to be re-recorded, but at the same time we had some severe problems with our management and instead this got released in demo format.

That's likely why his playing dominates the disc. Albrighton hoped to create a finished band version of the album later, but that never happened. Nor have we ever seen alternate versions or bonus tracks, though a two-CD edition in 2020 paired the album with Albrighton's solo work *The Follies of Rupert Treacle*. For more on that, see the Other Studio Recordings chapter at the end of this book.

Shortly before the album's release, Albrighton suggested to *Get Ready to Rock* that it would explore the most dubious of themes:

Book of Days will be a loose concept, basically revolving around present human situations, or perceptions of the present human lifestyle and all the positive/negative things it offers.

Unlike, I suppose, every other album ever made. In the same interview, he mentioned that his plans were 'an orchestrated version of *Journey*' and a new solo album, but the band's ongoing hassles stymied both prospects.

All songs composed by Albrighton.

'Over Krakatoa'

Our opening ambience isn't space for a change, but a simulation of high-altitude wind and the ominous roll of what sounds most like thunder, but is presumably the awakening volcano far beneath. According to the lyric, we're flying in a microlight aircraft high over the caldera and it's about to explode. The jaunt is part of a restless search for enlightenment that has also taken our singer Jonah-like into the depths, on a ship across the desert, and on a quest for the holy grail.

Musically, the track is the herald of a whole new Nektar sound, shoved right up there at the beginning of the disc to force us to accommodate it. Instead of mid-tempo funk, we have coruscating hard rock suffused in modern prog textures: clattery rim-shot percussion, rhythmic guitar slap, insane bass undulations, and a half-spoken, tuneless, and heavily distorted vocal. Even Albrighton's guitar solo has new mannerisms: high wild clusters alternating with snatches of scripted riffs. Once you get over the shock of the change, it's absolutely enthralling, a calling card for a band that has suddenly, as the lyric suggests, regained its sense of adventure and a reckless disregard for convention.

'King of the Deep'

The previous track alluded to whales – so here's a song dedicated to them. A female cetacean witnesses her children speared by whalers and sinks deep to find shelter. A male glides through the empty water, consoled by the knowledge that upstart man will likely be gone as quickly as he came: 'How sick we are,' Albrighton spits, 'to take a life 'til they're no more.'

The track begins with a daringly fast rock swagger, shoving manically against the wall of Steve Mattern's Hammond like a bodybuilder's gym on PCP. Then, as if signalled by Albrighton's lyric quoting the 'down, down, down' motif from *Recycled*, we drop into a timeless, sunless abyss where synths emulate more sound effects: the grunts and growling of whales. An acoustic guitar chases spirals through the depths, the band begins a hesitant neo-prog rhythm, and Albrighton plays a thick choral electric solo through a rack's worth of digital effects. The track culminates in a vast anthemic chorus to show that the band haven't quite abandoned their old symphonic style.

'Lamorna'

By far the shortest track on the disc at just 1:29, this is a shimmering solo guitar piece designed to show off the rich sound of Albrighton's semi-acoustic. I like to think of it as linking to 'King of the Deep' by evoking a

summer's day on the cliffs of Lamorna near the tip of Cornwall, England,
gazing out at the water – the opposite in feel to Tony Iommi's similarly
positioned but chilly interlude 'Laguna Sunrise' on Black Sabbath's *Vol. 4.*

'Doctor Kool'
The band's second-worst title (only 'Y Can't I B More Like U 2020' on *The
Other Side* is guaranteed to raise the hackles higher) may well label a track
you're determined to hate before you've even heard it. Awkward, then, that
at 11:10, it's not just the longest track on the album, but also Albrighton's
longest studio track *of all* since the golden age. In fact, in this whole era, only
the title track of *The Other Side* beats it at 14:03.

But you know what? The track's a blast, a bright slab of up-tempo commercial
rock that enables Albrighton to galumph through his most vicious putdown,
sinking his own scalpels into a fading beauty who relies on the plastic surgeon
of the title. As if on a youth kick of its own, the track's loaded with old
motifs: a big-hair AOR break, a funky guitar solo, a soaring refrain, touches of
acoustic guitar, even those baritone harmony vocals. It adds up to a highlight,
an insistent beat to provoke shape-throwing dance moves while something
spectacular shrills through your synapses like the good doctor's drugs.

'The Iceman'
Whereas it's hard to fold the derision of 'Doctor Kool' into Nektar's conceptual
continuity, 'The Iceman' is practically a sampler of Albrighton's recurring
targets. We're regaled here with disdain regarding a government run by 'Gates's
machines' (evoking the computer dystopia of *Recycled*), the 'rape' of the
natural world, rampant commercialism, even white privilege. The last links the
track tonally to Roy Harper's 'I Hate the White Man', but Harper would never
have prayed sincerely to God for a solution. Nor, probably, would he have
extrapolated all this bile out of so specific an event: then-President George W.
Bush's lifting of the ban on oil drilling in the Arctic National Wildlife Refuge.

The song is a curious hybrid of big box anthem rock and brooding
folk reminiscent of Bob Dylan's own putdown 'It's Alright Ma (I'm Only
Bleeding)'. Like Dylan, Albrighton declaims his tumbling imagery in a world-
weary monotone that stirs upward only on the penultimate note of each
line. Fittingly, too, his intonation sounds just like rock's other great snark:
Roger Waters. However, the track's sound world is well crafted, including
tinkling synths which evoke the glittering tundra of Alaska ('the State of 49'
as Albrighton calls it) and phase-shifting rhythms like frigid winds building
horizontal icicles on exposed derricks. In the central calm, synth voices keen
impotently over the mounds of butchered seals.

'Where Are You Now'
Big brassy slabs of fuzz guitar thicken this joyously energetic rocker, making
it even more perplexing that the lyric is so negative. Albrighton's verses are

a nod to *Remember the Future*, wondering what happened to the open road that the album seemed to represent. The title (with or without question mark) is directed at bluebird himself. Phrases such as 'don't you abandon me' sound like the blind boy grown to a man and looking back with regret at the failure he made of things. That's certainly not how I hope to leave that beloved album, so it's uncomfortable to consider this song canon.

A robust prog centre adds an insistent synth sequence and dramatic ensemble smash chords. The second half of the long (10:43) track consists of one lyrical Albrighton solo after another, each again in that fat fuzz style. If only the words matched the transcendence of the playing.

'Book of Days (Between the Lines)'
The last seven minutes of the album are a suite consisting of two equally sized acoustic ballads with all but identical titles. This first half introduces the conceit: our lives are books in which the lessons we learn and the emotions we feel are all written, page after page.

'Book of Days'
A shift of key (from D to A) lifts us into the second half's elaboration of the theme. Albrighton suggests that it's possible to share your life book with the one you love. There's a distinct Beatles feel to this part. Musically, we hear Lennon's distinctive sour chord changes over a steady, cello-like synth rhythm. Albrighton even plays a simple Harrison-style solo at the end. Lyrically, the song hinges around a direct quote of McCartney's phrase 'let it be'. (I'm not convinced the phrase 'look at me' is also meant as a nod).

The last verse ties everything up in a little knot of conceptual wonder. 'Close your eyes and you'll see,' Albrighton sings. Lennon could have written that, but the sentiment is pure Nektar.

A Spoonful of Time (2012)

Personnel:
Roye Albrighton: guitar, vocals
Klaus Henatsch: keyboards
Ron Howden: drums
Additional personnel:
Jürgen Engler: listed as 'additional instrumentation'
For guest musicians, see each individual track
Recorded: Atom H Studios, Austin, TX, USA (date unknown)
Producers: Jürgen Engler, Chris Lietz
Released: Purple Pyramid CD and LP, November 2012 (USA)
Running time: 1:09:29

In a list of the least compelling things Nektar could have done in 2012, I'm sure that a double LP of faithful cover versions must be close to the top. It wasn't a great idea, and though it was well executed, it remains the kind of release that makes fans cringe quietly inside, particularly since it held up a work in progress of new original songs. But all its guest stars gave it a fighting chance of achieving the one thing that new Nektar albums found it so hard to do: sell in quantity.

Nektar had become involved with the US label Cleopatra Records, one of whose subdivisions was Purple Pyramid. Cleopatra gained the band an outlet and a new manager, John Lappen. It also placed them among renegade company such as Brainticket (with whom they toured in 2011), Guru Guru, and Hawkwind. The first release of the deal was the *Retrospektive 1969–1980* compilation.

Purple Pyramid was also putting together the album *Songs of the Century: An All-Star Tribute to Supertramp* (released in 2012) under the auspices of Yes multi-instrumentalist and tribute album king Billy Sherwood. He'd already mustered up star turns for tributes to The Beatles, Genesis, Led Zeppelin, Rush, UFO, and many more, including a whole bunch of albums trying to hitch a ride on the skirts of Pink Floyd's vast fanbase. Playing along with Sherwood on *Songs of the Century* were the likes of Peter Banks, Geoff Downes, Larry Fast, Gary Green, Tony Kaye, and Rick Wakeman, with vocalists including Annie Haslam and John Wetton. Roye Albrighton was invited to participate. He provided vocals (no guitar) to 'Rudy', which at least had the distinction of coming from prog classic *Crime of the Century* (1974) even if it wasn't one of the hits.

Following on from this, Lappen suggested that Nektar do an album by themselves in which they would interpret a whole bunch of old songs. They didn't even need to choose their own tracks – indeed, Albrighton claimed they had no input into the content. He told *The Rocktologist* in 2014:

> I could name at least a dozen songs I would have preferred to copy or pay tribute to. It might be nice to do other songs that people know but haven't been covered.

But that wasn't the deal here. The deal was well-worn pop and rock standards played the Nektar way.

The band mustered up enthusiasm. The work was simple enough and there was scope for a little interpretation. But then that wasn't on the cards, either. Albrighton continued:

> Originally it was just going to be the core band doing covers. All of a sudden, they said: 'Let's get Steve Howe on it, John Wetton.' All these legendary musicians. I thought it wasn't really Nektar anymore.

The band were reduced to providing basic tracks with vocals, which they recorded in Jürgen Engler's studio. Engler then grafted on whatever guests he could persuade to contribute. There was no chance of prima donna rock stars messing up the studio, wasting time and money on endless retakes, or throwing huffy fits. There wasn't even any interaction. The whole thing was handled remotely. For a Rick Wakeman solo, say, all Engler needed to do was send a copy of the backing track over to Wakeman's studio and let him send back the results. Finally, the whole thing was mixed by Sherwood to bring out the best of each performance.

That was the way these all-star albums were made. It's no wonder Sherwood pumped out so many of them. Who wouldn't want to play along to a well-known song in the comfort of their home studio for a quick and easy buck? It made it possible to gather a whole rugby team of prog's brightest fading stars and they didn't even need to run out on the pitch together. *A Spoonful of Time* was full of people that Albrighton never actually met.

The strange title was surely not a Cream reference, even though Ginger Baker did appear on the set. Nor surely did it refer to *A Full Spoon of Seedy Blues*, *A Spoonful of Cathy Young*, the Lovin' Spoonful, Can's 'Spoon', or *Mary Poppins*. Perhaps it was meant to evoke Genesis's song 'Supper's Ready' (which includes the line 'a spoonful of miracle'), but there's no Genesis cover here. My feeling, given Sherwood's involvement, is that it was originally *A Saucerful of Time*, and perhaps even started life as yet another Pink Floyd tribute album, except the scope widened and the title needed to be altered to avoid confusion.

Nektar Play Pink Floyd – imagine that. The shame is that what we got was so much less.

'Sirius' (Parsons, Woolfson)

Guest musician: Michael Pinnella: keyboards

The Alan Parson's Project's crowd-rousing instrumental (appropriately enough from *Eye in the Sky*) is beefed up to an even more dramatic walk-on anthem featuring Pinnella's plump, guitar-like synth solo. However, it is a meandering piano cooldown that makes the track.

'Spirit of the Radio' (Peart, Lee, Lifeson)

Guest musician: Mark Kelly: keyboards

Nektar's screwed-up title (it should be 'The Spirit of Radio') never seems to have been corrected, so let's suppose nobody cared. There was no way Nektar could hope to emulate Rush's frantically agile tech rock (and however good he is, Howden ain't no Neil Peart) so even attempting a faithful recreation of this genre classic was a hiding to nowhere. Still, the band are game. Albrighton channels his best Geddy Lee vocal, and Marillion keyboard player Kelly steps up for squelchy synth burbles that sound like a million teenage spots all popping at once. The original's crazy changes toward the end are all in place, including those snatches of reggae that are carefully buried by Kelly's don't-look-there flights of sonic ping pong.

'Fly Like an Eagle' (Miller)

Guest musicians: Geoff Downes: keyboards, Joel Vandroogenbroeck: keyboards, flute

Yes join Brainticket – a very strange coupling indeed – on the bed of The Steve Miller Band's soft rock standard, which at least has the same kind of stop-start, white funk rhythm that Nektar themselves pioneered in the golden age, and the galactic, head-clearing synth runs that Vandroogenbroeck favoured. *A Spoonful of Time* ramps up the production and makes those head-spinning high spirals the track's highlight, played mostly by Vandroogenbroeck's trademark ethereal, reverb-drenched flute. Again Albrighton's vocal is a chameleon, but the keyboard jousts are the feature as each of the players attempts to out-psychedelicise the other – a party track for the band's partiest album.

'Wish You Were Here' (Waters, Gilmour)

Guest musician: Edgar Froese: keyboards

Any attempt to recreate something this beloved is surely sacrilege – but Nektar's version is the album's outstanding success. Albrighton's twin acoustic guitar introduction set against Froese's ghostly, hovering synth drones is sheer perfection. Yes, he sings just like David Gilmour, but the track's languid melancholy, slow as a clock finally running down, emphasises the fact that the original was created at a time of weariness so profound that *Wish You Were Here* could hardly rouse itself from the floor. While Froese's other major contribution is a clattery synth background, Albrighton grafts on a fierce flight of electric guitar seemingly to try to stun listeners out of this torpor – and it works. Toward the end the beat picks up for a satisfying cruise into the sunset of the fade.

'For the Love of Money' (Gamble, Huff, Jackson)

Guest musicians: Ian Paice: drums, Nik Turner: saxophone

Black soul trio The O'Jays may not be a band you instantly associate with prog's plunderable heritage, but this heartfelt reproduction of the group's slippery bass riff, smooth, slinking dance beat, and seductive sax break was anything but throwaway. At 7:41, it's the most substantial track on the album, showing that Nektar based their recreation on the seven-minute album version (on 1973's *Ship Ahoy*) rather than the half-size hit single. Whether they *should* cover a song off an album so racially sensitive is another matter, but Nektar were far from the first white musicians to appropriate the groove: Todd Rundgren had covered 'Money' way back in 1982. Nektar's take is a brassy wall of sound over which Turner lays great slabs of honk.

'Can't Find My Way Home' (Winwood)

Guest musicians: Mel Collins: flute, saxophone, Steve Howe: guitar, Derek Sherinian: keyboards

Blind Faith's pause for breath in its thunderous 1969 album is luminous, personal, and instantly relatable for anyone who has drunk or smoked too much to know which street to take, so decides that sitting on the kerb is a viable alternative. Nektar's version ditches the sad-sack introspection for a befuddling overproduction that sees the band and their three superfluous guests all vying to add notes to every available space. Albrighton manages somehow to pitch his voice in that sliver of differentiation between Steve Winwood's and Eric Clapton's vocal style, while Mel Collins injects runs of woodwinds that sound like nothing so much as Winwood's bandmate Chris Wood. The harmony chorus is a mess.

'2000 Light Years from Home' (Jagger, Richards)

Guest musician: Simon House: violin

Ancient, creaky, and surely misplaced, the album's oldest cover (from The Rolling Stones' maligned 1967 album *Their Satanic Majesties Request*) is a fitting touch paper for Nektar's own outer space rocket flights, containing as it does that stunningly evocative opening line and a sense of cosmic angst that was stolen from Pink Floyd and flung straight back in the UFO scene's face so effectively that I'm sure it influenced not just Van der Graaf Generator (its own 'Pioneers Over C' has the same nonchalant desolation) but Hawkwind, Gong, and Nektar themselves: *Journey to the Centre of the Eye* in microcosm.

In tribute, then, Nektar pile on the late-period psychedelia for all it's worth, swamping the song in a sludge of Hawkwind electronics that make House's fiddle squalls righteously appropriate. Here's an alternative universe we never experienced but which, on this evidence, I long to abscond to, one in which Nektar remained a space rock band and are even now sharing festival stages with bands of that style to crowds of elderly, naked people on mushrooms flinging themselves in mud puddles. As it is, the 2011 Space Rock Invasion tour with Brainticket is no substitute (see the Live Recordings chapter at the end of this book for more). Trippy, for sure, but not as mind manifesting as it ought to have been, and this '2000 Light Years' isn't even half the length it deserves.

'Riders on the Storm' (Densmore, Manzarek, Krieger, Morrison)
Guest musicians: Rod Argent: keyboards, Billy Sheehan: bass
Jim Morrison's evocation of the Charles Manson of the mind, oozing snakelike across the hot blacktop of the LA night, is translated here to a pounding rock ballad that sounds like Blue Öyster Cult's 'Fire of Unknown Origin' played at the wrong speed – an ouroboros joined. Prosody sticklers should rejoice that Albrighton manages to phrase 'take a long holiday' correctly. Everyone else can be astounded by Argent's drop-dead perfect old school prog rock organ solo. Somebody give that man a band of his own.

'Blinded by the Light' (Springsteen)
Guest musicians: Ginger Baker: drums, Joakim Svalberg: keyboards
It's not Springsteen's own stream of lunatic consciousness that is celebrated here but Manfred Mann's Earth Band's 1977 hit reinvention of the word splurge as pomp rock masterwork. Opeth's Svalberg provides a bright, unfussy reproduction of all the riffs and rhythms, including the rendition of 'Chopsticks'.

   Baker appears to be onboard, but I hear nothing in the drumming that distinguishes him. Albrighton squeals on wah-wah guitar in between the incomprehensible syllables and sings in his very best Eric Clapton impersonation, perhaps to make Baker feel at home. He follows the Earth Band's script so faithfully he even engages in the same humorous mispronunciation of 'deuce'.

'Out of the Blue' (Ferry, Manzanera)
Guest musician: Simon House: violin
A Roxy Music track from *Country Life* which *somebody* in the production team must have thought was a winner. Though it's played straight, there was no way Albrighton could reproduce Bryan Ferry's psychotic airline pilot mannerisms, instead coming across less like a cockpit Patrick Bateman than David Bowie moonlighting as a trolley dolly. But House was a good match for Eddie Jobson's crazed, phase-swamped violin blast, which here appears to have been plugged through the lousiest amp in the studio.

'Old Man' (Young)
Guest musician: David Cross: violin
For the most part, Neil Young songs are too personal to translate well. This *Harvest* highlight is one of a clutch of songs Young wrote to celebrate having used his *After The Gold Rush* earnings to buy himself a big ranch in Redwood City, and was specifically addressed to the old caretaker that came along with the acreage. Nektar's version must, of necessity, ditch all Young's plaintive authenticity (Albrighton, wisely, doesn't try to sound like him) and so is rendered neuter. Additionally, Cross's electric violin makes it excruciatingly sweet.

'Dream Weaver' (Wright)

Guest musician: Jerry Goodman: violin

Gary Wright's original is a shimmering soft rock delight, satiny with electric piano and studded, star-like, with ethereal synth sparkles. Both the theme and the gentle funk rhythm are suited to Nektar, the former due to Albrighton's solo album on the same subject, *The Follies of Rupert Treacle* (see the Other Recordings chapter at the end of this book for more). This rendition uses sumptuous Mellotron samples in place of the electric piano and Goodman's high violin slides to help evoke the falling stars, but it is indeed close to Nektar's contemporary work in both style and subject.

'I'm Not in Love' (Stewart, Gouldman)

Guest musicians: Joel Vandroogenbroeck: flute, Rick Wakeman: keyboards

It's an impossible task to emulate 10cc's tape choir, so the band lay the piece on thick synth textures. Howden's jazz rock rhythm is a misfire, but Vandroogenbroeck manages to fling the track in a completely different direction with his flute trills, turning the aching ambivalence of uncommitted love into a remarkable head space in which you don't care about the emotion whatsoever with all those dancing pixies in your brain.

I'm guessing that Wakeman adds the busy piano work under the verses. He certainly adds the vintage 'Close to the Edge' style synth runs during the breaks. That's what they pay him for. There's an uncredited feminine voice to whisper the 'Be quiet, big boys don't cry' insert.

'Africa' (Paich, Porcaro)

Guest musicians: Bobby Kimball: vocals, Patrick Moraz: keyboards, Joel Vandroogenbroeck: flute, sitar

Just as you're yelling at the band to leave the song alone, here comes a scoop: original Toto singer Bobby Kimball is roped in to sing 'Africa' – and what a relief it is. Albrighton relegates himself to beefing up Kimball's breathless phrasing in the choruses.

Sincere it might have been in 1982, but the song's tourist-level appropriation of African themes has granted it an uncomfortable legacy that surely Nektar must have been aware of 30 years later. The song provokes conflicting feelings of PC responsibility versus guilty pleasure that make Vandroogenbroeck's ethnic flute playing and Moraz's marimba-style synths even more of a problem. Of course, Vandroogenbroeck had toyed with the Africa of the foreigner's imagination since Brainticket's *Celestial Ocean* in 1974, and it would be a thankless task to try to list all the prog bands who wove African drumming into their sound, some to great effect. Jade Warrior, in particular, were immersed in world music years before Paul Simon's so-called innovation, and had the cachet of an association with one of Britain's true African prog rock groups: Assagai. Nektar – well, Nektar did not, and so 'Africa' comes across as a slightly distasteful pastiche.

Oh yes, and then there are Vandroogenbroeck's delightful sitar touches – but we won't go there.

Alternate versions and bonus tracks

In the same year as the physical release, Nektar put out a download-only 'deluxe edition' comprising the full album, plus instrumental versions of all 14 of its tracks – essentially a classic rock karaoke set.

There are no Who songs on *A Spoonful of Time*, but I would wager that the band's version of 'Baba O'Riley' was recorded in the same sessions. The track was released instead on *Who Are You: An All Star Tribute to The Who* the same year. That album attributes the piece to Albrighton and Howden alone (no Henatsch), plus once again Jürgen Engler on 'additional instrumentation'. The guest, in this case, was Jerry Goodman, who also appeared on one track on *Spoonful*.

'Baba O'Riley' (Townshend)

Guest musician: Jerry Goodman: violin

Riveting but carbon-copy synth patterns and by-the-numbers rhythm section set up Albrighton's note-perfect Roger Daltrey impersonation. The track's main distinguisher is its vast, near-saturated sound field on the big power chords. Goodman's contribution is mostly just to reproduce the gypsy rave-up in the fade, which he does adequately and facelessly.

Time Machine (2013)

Personnel:
Roye Albrighton: guitar, lead vocals
Klaus Henatsch: keyboards
Ron Howden: drums, vocals
Billy Sherwood: bass
Recorded: Sherwood Studios, Los Angeles, CA, USA (date unknown)
Producers: Roye Albrighton, Billy Sherwood
Released: Purple Pyramid CD, June 2013 (USA)
Running time: 1:06:37

The last studio album of Albrighton's career took years to arrive. It was promoted in the *Retrospektive 1969–1980* booklet in 2011 under the title *Juggernaut*. The same year, Albrighton told *Guitar International*:

> Mostly the songs are written in sections. I usually just keep playing around with an idea until I feel it sits right and then take it from there. This could be on any instrument, not just guitar. For example, a track from the forthcoming album was conceived on the bass guitar.

But *A Spoonful of Time* was wedged in the way. Afterwards, Albrighton seemed to adopt Billy Sherwood's way of working, as he told *The Rocktologist* in 2014:

> These days, I write the songs and I do pre-production. I play everything. I play keyboards, guitar, and sing. I sent these recordings to Billy and he put the bass on. Then we all went over [to his studio] and all we had to do was put [on] fresh vocals, drums, and a few keyboards bits, and it was ready. The whole album was done in nine days.

This new, more casual way of working was reflected in the album itself, which lacked a uniting theme or musical pretensions. 'It covers a lot of situations that we might find ourselves in at any particular time in our lives,' Albrighton told *Something Else!* in 2012, repeating that meaningless *Book of Days* spiel.

When it finally came, the CD version was definitive and is the one detailed here. There was a truncated LP consisting of 'A Better Way', 'If Only I Could', and 'Time Machine' on the A-side and 'Tranquility', 'Mocking The Moon', 'Juggernaut', and 'Diamond Eyes' on the B-side, all at CD length. There have never been alternate versions or bonus tracks, and no singles were released.

The set was received with great enthusiasm from the community. *Prog* hailed its 'circuitous, magically meandering structures' and Albrighton's 'unconventionally thrilling guitar work...his crescendos are bejewelled with brilliance', summarising it as 'a treasury of idiosyncratic gems' and a

'wondrous blend of perverse three-point turns and sheer emotional heft'
– but it has not settled into a fan favourite. You may also note all those
oddity qualifiers in *Prog*'s review, which likely indicate that the reviewer still
considers the band outside the prog rock mainstream.

Albrighton enthused to *The Rocktologist*:

> I really like it because it has lots of different styles of music on it. You have a
> ballad, power rock, it's jazzy here and there. There are also big, long pieces
> – ten minutes – for the prog fans. It's a good all-round album.

It kicked off something of a resurgence for the group, which was at last
bedding into prog's reawakening. Bands of various perturbations toured the
album, including a spot on Yes's Cruise To The Edge in 2013, presumably
at Billy Sherwood's instigation. Because of the sheer bulk of Nektar's back
catalogue and their wish to perform a hefty selection of the new material,
there was almost no time for any of the old improvisations. The musicians
had to play all the highlights each night and snatch space for what they
hoped were classics to come. But Albrighton was beginning to feel himself
at home in the new firmament, a bastion of rock's legendary years, and
regardless of the negativity that suffuses *Time Machine,* there was a warm
smile on his face every time he stepped out on the stage, right up to the
end.

All songs composed by Albrighton except where marked.

'A Better Way'

The album's introduction is a wallowing, dark ambient sequence with high
sonar blips over which we tap into a telephone conversation between a
hapless man and a demonic version of himself, signalling that this is to be an
album of uncomfortable introspection. And indeed, in this song, we witness
Albrighton staring nakedly at himself at a point so late in his career. 'Seems
like I've been here before,' he sighs, 'singing the same old song.' But it's not
so bad. What keeps the man in the mirror battling onward is the child he sees
behind his eyes.

The music belays any self-doubts. A storming start merges thick, almost tech
metal with soaring symphonic touches. Howden pounds at his toms so hard
you can see the dust of old habits billowing off the skins. Then, a little over
halfway through its 9:17 running time, all this dissolves into an acoustic guitar
piece over synth strings. This gradually coalesces into drifting prog, over
which we hear a *third* spoken voice – with heavy intimations of Mike Pinder's
recitations of Graeme Edge's poems in peak period Moody Blues – reassuring
us that past time may be immutable, but the future is still open to endless
possibilities so long as we remain young at heart. The reward for squirming
through this sermon is an anthemic ending with staircase-climbing vocals and
squalls of electric guitar.

'Set Me Free, Amigo'

A brightly commercial rocker with exactly the Mexican accents you'd fear.
Such storytelling pastiche isn't really Nektar, but Albrighton romps through
his tall tale of a bank-robbing bandit who ends up in a dirty jail cell
wondering if it's all just a dream out of 'some cowboy magazine.' In other
words, if this second phase Nektar, too, is just a young boy's fantasy that
Albrighton has been deluding himself with ever since. While you're pondering
that, revel in the eye-rolling excess of the track's climactic Mariachi synths,
the dizziest appropriation of the culture since ELO's 'Across the Border'.

'Destiny'

Albrighton is still in front of the mirror for this unfussy power ballad
which hits the expected beats, passing through a sequence of introspective
Mellotron-type synths before the inevitable big, boxy redemption at the end:
'I'm trying to hide in my masquerade,' he confesses. But even though life
hasn't worked out the way he hoped it would, he's survived all the downs. It's
impossible not to view the song as an autobiographical remembrance of that
long period out of the limelight following *Man in the Moon*. 'I have to admit
that I'd almost quit,' Albrighton tells us, but 'I was thrown a line,' saved both
personally and artistically.

'If Only I Could'

Despite the more personal Albrighton we've witnessed so far on the
album, some old obsessions have not worn themselves smooth. Here's yet
another entry in the Nektar strand of anti-pollution diatribes. Musically, it's
adept pomp rock built on a sound pool of ringing fingerpicked guitar and
Henatsch's piano flourishes, but lyrically we've been here before. The ice caps
are melting, cars are belching out poison, and all the singer wants to do is
wash his face clean of 'all trace of the human race' as if he's not a part of this
collective madness.

But *something's* new. There's regret here, too, an acknowledgement that
the attempts Albrighton made to change people's minds – he means through
Nektar's previous albums – have been a 'powerless parade.' But that's the
thing about message songs. Their effect is hardly quantifiable, and even
the most commercial music has proven to be all but impotent to reform the
millions who heard it. A whole world listened to The Beatles, yet the wars
never stopped. Albrighton may well wonder if he should have ditched the
niche rock for mainstream pop so he could get his word out to more people,
but honestly, it wouldn't have made any difference.

'Time Machine'

Sherwood's chunky, note-bending bass, Albrighton's guitar harmonics,
Howden's rim-sharp snare, and Henatsch's over-busy Hammond solo all bring
Yes to mind, suggesting the bassist had more influence on the sound than

just his studio. The song rouses to fat-cheeked, dramatic choruses that are its weakest point, as if it's straining too much to be an epic – the piece being about twice as long (at 8:07) as it needs to be. Nor is Albrighton's lyric his best. The time machine we're all living in is simply time itself, always moving forward, and hence we're always 'livin' on the edge' in both senses of the word, warriors of life without a clue of what's careering our way next.

'Tranquility'
This is a truly weird song. It reiterates 'If Only I Could' in the first verse – the sea levels are rising, and we're all to blame – but then suggests that the ocean can be solace and escape, if only in our minds. This dubious suggestion is set, not to the burbling drift its opening suggests, another evocation of Jimi Hendrix's fish-nodding depths, but to pummelling power pop. Indeed, there's a disconcerting dissonance in hearing Albrighton's soothing intonation of the title set against Howden's most manic drumming. It was obviously designed that way, but it simply doesn't work.

'Mocking the Moon' (Craven, Henatsch)
A bright-eyed but merely space-filling ballad in which the writer raises a sardonic toast to the moon for sitting up there so far from all the world's storms and troubles, only to find it smiling benignly down on him. We've heard the voice of the moon before in the title track of *Man in the Moon*, but here it is again without that horrible octave drop effect. Yes, I'm far away from all that, the moon says, but I *do* shine down on you all, helping to guide your steps onward.

'Talk to Me' (Howden)
In what seems like the second part of a band's support program to gee up its despondent leader, Howden has solace of his own to impart to a remarkably modern-sounding synth backing. Albrighton responds with the album's best guitar solo.

'Juggernaut'
The original title track isn't that expansive an instrumental (it's just 4:37), but it presents a fine set of contemporary prog changes. You can sense the whole band revelling in its funky complexities, meaning it's such a jolt when the piece suddenly slams to a halt mid-groove. Still, there's space for fiddly Henatsch solos on electric piano and synth alongside meaty riffs on Albrighton's fuzz guitar, though his own solo is in a clean jazz style.

'Diamond Eyes'
The longest track (at 10:14), and the album's shot at a classic, is a return to the symphonic metal of the opener, with the same J-shaped trajectory as so

many prog classics: fast opening section, long slow middle, and mid-tempo triumphal ending that blasts the roof off. It's an excellent, driving base upon which you'd hope for the archetypal pomp rock story of hope, setback, and redemption.

That's not what we get. 'Diamond Eyes' is a vehicle for Albrighton's bitterest, most world-weary lyric. The song is a warning of the allure of fame, whose hypnotising promises of 'livin' your dreams' will sucker you, destroy you, and leave you a dried-up husk. It's a sour way to summarise a career – it's hard to see how the singer could move onward to new albums after this – which makes it so galling that here is where we will always leave the man, broken and crying at all his wrecked promise.

The Other Side (2020)

Personnel:
Ryche Chlanda: guitar, lead vocals
Randy Dembo: bass, 12-string guitar
Ron Howden: drums, vocals
Derek 'Mo' Moore: bass, vocals
Kendall Scott: keyboards
Recorded: 2019 at Shorefire Recording Studio, Long Branch, NJ, USA
Producer: Benjamin Meade
Released: Cosmic Cowboy Records LP (USA), Esoteric Antenna CD (Europe), 2020
Running time: 1:06:05

The splintering of Nektar into two competing factions in 2018 was notionally the latest replay of the band's recurring dichotomy, the gulf between those who wished to centre operations in the US and those who wished to ground them in Germany. In this case, original members Moore, Howden, and Brockett formed the US contingent, while the Europeans boasted not just a set of latter-day members, but the spiritual heir to the first manifestation of that dichotomy in the form of Albrighton's son Che, who had played with the band in 2014.

According to Moore, Howden was the instigator of the split, and Henatsch its cause. When Albrighton died in 2016, the band consisted of himself, Howden, Henatsch, and bassist Tom Fry. The latter three continued much as Nektar had continued in 1976, bringing in a new guitarist/vocalist, Alex Hoffmeister. The plan was that this group would move seamlessly on to maintain the momentum they had built up in Albrighton's final years. But when Henatsch declared himself de facto leader and decision maker in 2018, Howden bailed.

In the US, Howden shrewdly approached Moore and, through him, Brockett – neither of whom had had any involvement with Nektar for about 16 years – to form a band of their own. Practically by definition, this made Henatsch's version the 'new' (younger, more forward-looking, less legacy) Nektar, whereas Howden, Moore, and Brockett ironically represent the tribute band route: transfixed on old songs and past glories. Moore repeatedly told interviewers that he considered *The Other Side* the follow-up to *Recycled*, as he explained to *At the Barrier* in 2020:

> I would place *The Other Side* after *Recycled* in our legacy/catalogue. It is the *only* concept album to follow *Recycled* and has the 1970s feel about it.

Henatsch didn't think the same of his new disc *Megalomania*. He thought of it as the next album after *Time Machine*, the creation of a band stepping ahead even if that meant antagonising the old band's members. 'The baton has been passed' to Henatsch, its press release claimed. And indeed, isn't this the very tenet that drives prog rock – the very meaning of the word? You progress, or you ossify. You stay young, or you close the coffin lids on the band. The issue is whether the name New Nektar creates enough distance to signal those progressive intentions, or whether using the N-word at all implies a marketing calculation.

That this might be true of both incarnations is a sore point. Tireless PR work by Moore has made him the official voice of the Nektar brand, and indeed it is this band that gains most of the column inches. It helps, too, that *The Other Side* garnered favourable reviews, whereas those for *Megalomania* have been dismal.

In the previous chapter, I mentioned that Nektar were bedding into the new prog landscape at the time of Albrighton's death. The question with heritage acts is what they actually represent: are you there for the songs or the personalities? Does it matter, for a band whose richest legacy is its early work, that there are no original members, so long as the songs are played well and the lights look great? Is legitimacy merely a state of mind? Indeed, in this age of digital avatars of old pop and rock stars, do you care at all who's on the stage so long as you have a good time?

There's no simpler demonstration of prog's legacy/progression issue than the tour that the US incarnation of Nektar kicked off in September 2021. Dubbed 'Vinyl Sides Live', its aim was to pull in the punters by promising a night of golden age classics. 'Audiences will be treated to entire album sides from some of Nektar's epic recordings,' declared the press release. That means discs up to *Recycled*. The shows also included material from the new album *The Other Side*, skipping just about everything in between.

To be fair to those skipped years, album sides were always the band standard. They had consistently played 'A Tab in the Ocean' and the first sides of *Remember the Future* and *Recycled*. But the backward focus also meant a return to old values: Nektar would improvise every night, just like they used to. Moore declared to *VWMusic* in 2021:

> We listened to our fans, who were always asking for more and more old pieces of music. We learned more, including the entire new album, all of *A Tab in the Ocean*, all of *Remember the Future*, all of *Recycled*, and a big chunk of *...Sounds Like This* and *Down to Earth*.

The Other Side wasn't just a spiritual return to the 1970s. It even sounded like an old, classic LP. With CDs waning and a thriving vinyl resurgence, it was formatted that way: the double disc splatter vinyl LP version is certainly definitive in this case (though LP and CD have identical contents save for different mastering styles), consisting of a *Sounds* distribution of tracks. *Sounds* was organised 3-2-2-2 across its four sides. *The Other Side* is 2-2-2-3. And the Wenske cover image looks of a piece with *Sounds*, complete with staring eyes.

To create it, the band dug into its songbook for live gems and unfinished pieces from the golden age. As Moore told *Hollywood Soapbox* in 2019:

A lot of the music came from sessions in my basement in 1978 that Ryche [Chlanda] and I put together, and we brought them all out. And we spruced them all up, and we have an album that is 68 minutes long.

An even older piece, the Albrighton tribute 'The Devil's Door', samples the live version of the song from Bielefeld in June 1974 that had already been released on *Door to the Future* in 2005 (see the Live Recordings chapter at the end of this book for more), giving the album a fitting sense of being twin to Pink Floyd's memorial *The Endless River*. 'We feel that Roye was with us [in the studio],' Moore told *Prog* in 2020.

When it came to recording, Nektar followed the *Sounds* ethos of playing as much as possible live, but now with access to Pro Tools to edit, shape, and organise the jams, treating the source materials as building blocks to be crafted into a finished patchwork of sections. Effectively, the work of splicing and sequencing song fragments into larger structures that would have been conducted in band rehearsals for an album like *Remember,* was now handled afterwards on the computer. Only as the pieces progressed in this way did Moore and Brockett write the majority of the lyrics.

Moore claims that *The Other Side* is a narrative concept album – and if so, it's the first since *Remember* – though he has been sketchy about the story, preferring that listeners build their own from the components provided. He told *Prog*:

If you listen to the double album in the order that we have it you get a story. If you change the order around you get a different story. The idea is to use your imagination.

The basic intention, as far as I can figure it, seems to be this: a man and a woman ('wife/girlfriend/mother or whoever') love each other ('I'm on Fire'), but then she dies. He learns to fly, perhaps only in his imagination, so that he can write messages to her in the clouds ('Skywriter'). Eventually, he sets off on a long solo flight to try to find her ('The Other Side') and winds up 'floating in space' ('Drifting'). He finds himself at the entrance to hell ('Devils Door', without a definite article or apostrophe on the album sleeve) but turns away to 'The Light Beyond'. Finally, he sees the woman's eyes looking back at him, with true Nektar conceptual continuity, and they are reunited not just as people but as a spiritual unity. The album ends with a sermon, 'Y Can't I B More Like U 2020', a Roger Waters-style plea for more connection in *this* world rather than wait until it's too late. That year check in the title, I presume, doesn't just mean 'now' but refers to 20/20 vision.

A journey to death, then, and to a love that transcends death. Not particularly something you'd want to play on psychedelic drugs, but a lot less depressing than *Journey to the Centre of the Eye*.

Except for Moore and Brockett's lyrics, there are no writer credits on the album. I've listed all the current band members in alphabetical order, even for 'The Light Beyond', which consists instrumentally of only Scott's keyboards, and credited 'Devils Door' solely to the original band, though its lyric has been reworked.

'I'm on Fire' (Brockett, Chlanda, Dembo, Howden, Moore, Scott)

The moment the chunky, Deep Purple Hammond starts up, you know this is a classic-minded ride, and indeed it doesn't disappoint. To a mid-tempo metal roar, Nektar add huge chord changes, abrupt guitar flourishes, a constantly mutating instrumental centrepiece, along with Moore's rough, guttural lead vocal to demonstrate, over more than eight insistent minutes, a band balancing the weight of old age and the energy of youth.

Surprisingly, all this dramatic thrust is used, not to foretell the downfall of the world as *old* Nektar would have done, but to accompany a simple lyric about sexual desire. Since it's apparently a setting of Moore's real-life youthful sentiments to the woman who would become his wife, we're off to a perplexing start. 'I'm On Fire' blends reality with the album's narrative to suggest that *The Other Side* is as much a band autobiography as a fantasy tale, but it's an odd place to begin a cycle about love and redemption. It works only if you're aware of the real-life tale behind it – and that knowledge makes the album dangerously personal.

'Skywriter' (Brockett, Chlanda, Dembo, Howden, Moore, Scott)

Moore's concept of 'a guy who loses his girlfriend and is up in the sky writing letters to her', is here crystallised in a cinematic power ballad with a singalong chorus and synth textures that evoke a Beatles string quartet. Chlanda's lighter, less throaty voice is well suited to the song's subject, but the sheer heft of its production means it's not as airy as it intends. Scott's Hammond and Chlanda's electric guitar take turns evoking rising thermals without actually managing to get the track off the ground.

'Love Is'

Filling the second side of the LP version, the pairing of this and 'The Other Side' are given as a single track on the cover, though there's a clear transition between the two which means they're not even a suite, simply two pieces segued together – the lyric sheet, indeed, lists them separately.

At just 3:54 (the second shortest track on the album), this first part functions mostly as a prelude. It's old-school big production pop reminiscent of Jeff Lynne's Beatles reunion, built from flitters of synth and shimmering acoustic guitar chords that soon give way to Moore's weighty bass growls and

Chlanda's swooping slide guitar. The lyric is again simple, an expression of aching love for a person who has gone away. 'Love will smile at me through your eyes,' Chlanda sings, reinventing Nektar's eternal theme as a longing to emerge from the darkness of loss.

'The Other Side' (Brockett, Chlanda, Dembo, Howden, Moore, Scott)

The album's epic is not what you might suppose: a chance for a tricky prog workout. Instead, it's straightforward melodic pop for most of its 14:03 running time. The first half is lifted only by an understated Mellotron-like synth sample, some subtle rhythmic complexity, and a very brief set of ensemble changes. But the second half is much more interesting. Scott's piano sets up a slower, more contemplative sequence in which Chlanda plays a shimmering, weightless solo. The band gradually builds momentum under this – though Moore's bass is never less than monstrous – headed back to a final pop verse and a satisfying piano coda.

The lyric proposes that the narrator's quest to be reunited with his love should be read not just as a physical journey but as a trip through music itself, that playing and singing are a means of connection even beyond the separation of death. The idea was proposed by a line in 'Love Is': 'Can you hear when I play music?' Just like writing messages in the clouds for the deceased to see in 'Skywriter', so the music we play can reach the ones we've lost and, just maybe, wherever they are they will sing along.

'Drifting' (Brockett, Chlanda, Dembo, Howden, Moore, Scott)

This track also defies expectations, at least to begin with. You know exactly what a piece called 'Drifting' is supposed to evoke, but instead, it is the opposite: a return of the ponderous, elephantine stomp of the opener, all room-shuddering, minor key guitar chords and Howden's most megalithic drumming. When it settles, it is to hunks of Pink Floyd synth over a slow-motion bass riff, Dembo's disconcerting *second* bass flourishes, and an enormous wah-wah solo by Chlanda.

Alone of the album's tracks, the piece was left essentially as it was played live in the studio. There are minimal overdubs, mainly a perfunctory vocal. It's the set's greatest success, a nine-minute-wide canvas on which the band paints a solitary human figure, tiny and storm-tossed, flung among buffets of clouds and the shouting mouths of sunbeams with no earth to ground him.

'Devils Door' (Albrighton, Howden, Freeman, Moore)

The opening of the track is taken directly from the Bielefeld tape, panning Albrighton's unaccompanied guitar wildly back and forth across the channels, but it is the modern band that slams in to accompany him. In working with the restriction of the old tape, the band is forced to play to its tempo, with its spry changes and lightness of touch – consequently, it's the album's most affecting track. However, as a found object, included by Moore and Howden as a tribute to their fallen partner, it has nothing inherently to do with the album's narrative. Even with the awkwardly rewritten lyric, the door to hell is irrelevant to the cosmic search for a loved one who most certainly does not reside within. Rather, it comes across as a diversion, a window through which we view a different kind of story in progress. Sadly, that window does not allow us to catch more than a glimpse of Albrighton, and we certainly do not hear him singing to us as you'd think he should.

'The Light Beyond' (Chlanda, Dembo, Howden, Moore, Scott)

Opening side four, this tiny (2:51) instrumental represents 'the light that you see before you die' according to Moore. It consists of a spritely patchwork of synth strings that plays out exactly like the pretend string quartet of 'Skywriter'. Alas that the budget didn't stretch to a real orchestra, which would have lifted the track and the emotional heft of this part of the album immensely. There's a brief babble of voices – Moore identifies them as 'the voices of the dead' – before the track spirals skyward on waves of synth glitter.

'Look Thru Me' (Brockett, Chlanda, Dembo, Howden, Moore, Scott)

Interesting that at this climactic moment, the album's emotional core, the band chooses to keep the count in, shifting you out of the narrative and into the vérité of a band performing in the studio – a peek at the machinery. Treasure it: that's Nektar trying to make a connection with you.

What follows is less direct. 'Look Thru Me' entangles the set's most elaborate lyric in a labyrinthine arrangement of piano and acoustic guitar, leaving you little mental space to assimilate all the information you're bombarded with. In essence, the song tells the listener to try to see the real person inside the irrelevant shell of flesh and bone they wear.

Though all that busywork means it doesn't penetrate as deeply as it should, there's an affecting synth solo to focus upon: a shockingly clear electronic line cutting through all the wood and wires.

'Y Can't I B More Like U 2020' (Brockett, Chlanda, Dembo, Howden, Moore, Scott)

The more myopic critics linked this title, the band's most crass, with Prince, but it comes from a long line of song titles that try to look like they were spray-canned by dyslexic kids in a hurry. The most notorious purveyor of these was British pop band Slade, which Nektar may well have remembered from their golden age. Slade's titles were the intellectual equivalent of the skinhead cuts and bovver boots the band sported in their early days. A more relevant link musically is Blue Öyster Cult, whose rabble-pleasing 'R. U. Ready 2 Rock' was one of the lesser tracks on its overlooked classic *Spectres* (1978). BÖC's use of the slang form was specifically intended to make this most intellectual of metal bands (that's actually a link to Karel Čapek in the opening letters!) seem one with the kids in the stadium crowds, and the same is true here.

It's a delight, then, that the song isn't nearly as bad as the title it's been saddled with. It starts with a whole minute of Dembo's 12-string guitar in isolation, providing all the headroom the last track denied us, then shifts to electric piano for a powerful ballad in which Chlanda, surely purposefully, affects all Albrighton's vocal mannerisms. At the halfway mark, the track shifts gears into a fine sequence of prog stylings, providing everything we associate with Nektar, past and present, except their trademark scorched-foot funk.

Alternate versions and bonus tracks
To drum up interest for their new work, in 2019, Nektar released a single on 12-inch splatter vinyl – their first single on any medium since 2005 – comprising the album versions of 'Skywriter' and 'Devils Door'. This was designed to be sold at the New Jersey festival Progstock that October, where Nektar performed in a second billing to that other great insect band, SAGA. Their setlist premiered 'Skywriter', 'Drifting', and the new version of 'Devils Door'.

In 2021 the band released an expanded *The Other Side* on CD, which included a 'radio edit' of 'Skywriter' and a bonus DVD consisting of a documentary on the making of the album – the footage of the band playing live in the studio is priceless – and the rather faceless video of 'Drifting' they had created to promote it on Youtube.

Other Studio Recordings

This chapter lists only additional audio that has been made available to buy on physical formats, omitting rare and variant studio tracks on the band's website and circulating among fans.

The Boston Tapes

By the time Albrighton joined Prophecy in November 1969, the band had already begun stockpiling the music that would fuel their first four albums and enable their shift away from cover versions in live performance. The first of the Nektar songs they wrote was 'Good Day'. Many more followed swiftly in those early months. Albrighton himself brought more, including 'New Day Dawning', which he'd originally written for Rainbows.

As we receive the band in the discography I detailed in the bulk of this book, they seemed to arrive fully formed, not just with a singular sound, but with a narrative concept album for their first release. No other long-lasting British prog band of the period leaped out of the gate so dramatically. Barclay James Harvest, Caravan, Jethro Tull, The Moody Blues, Pink Floyd, Procol Harum, Renaissance, Soft Machine, Van der Graaf Generator, and Yes all worked up to their mature sound. Others like Camel, ELP, Gentle Giant, and King Crimson had already paid their apprenticeship on earlier albums. Nektar came out of nowhere.

I don't think West Germany is instrumental in this case. The country's labels accommodated a lot of risky material, but so did the British underground labels in the wake of *A Saucerful of Secrets*. However we receive them now, debut albums such as *Mercator Projected* and *It'll All Work Out in Boomland* were gutsy releases, and the progressive feeding frenzy produced a host of extraordinary bands that could have made it big. Nektar was lucky to have a producer and a studio that could nurture an untried band with a challenging sound, but I believe they could have managed the same on Deram, Harvest, or Vertigo.

Besides, there *was* an apprenticeship of a kind. Counting their origin as November 1969, it took more than 18 months before Nektar entered the studio to record *Journey to the Centre of the Eye*, an eternity in any market at the time. It's just that all the work happened under the rock radar. And there was an earlier album, too, though in common with other bands that seemed to arrive suddenly, such as Blue Öyster Cult, it wasn't released until decades later.

It's hard to parse just how Nektar would have sounded had somebody actually released what we now know as *The Boston Tapes*: 41 minutes of rough-hewn sound that unbalances the discography as given. It's much like wondering what Pink Floyd would have sounded like if they'd made an album for ESP-Disk in mid-1966 – and believe it or not, that came close to happening. The tape contains early readings of 'New Day Dawning', 'Do You Believe in Magic?', and 'Good Day', which presumably would not then have been available for ...*Sounds Like This*. It also predominantly consists of love

121

songs, including a version of Brian Hyland's 1962 hit 'Sealed with a Kiss' (written by Peter Udell and Gary Geld) that would break Nektar's boast of never putting covers on their early studio albums. A boast that's not quite true anyway, given the uncredited steal from 'Norwegian Wood' on *Sounds*.

The recording happened due to a chance encounter with Charlie Dreyer, an also-ran Boston producer who at the time had been involved in a handful of American releases, most notably Flat Earth Society's 1968 album *Waleeco*. His claim to fame was as an engineer on early 1970s albums for Mason Proffitt and Janis Ian. He also owned the label that put out The Shaggs' *Philosophy of the World* in 1969, though that's likely not company you'd wish Nektar to keep. Better, perhaps, to think of the group alongside excellent Bosstown Sound bands such as Ultimate Spinach and Earth Opera, though the scene's star had plummeted to a crater full of cinders by 1970.

Dreyer caught Nektar's act in West Germany and invited the members over to Boston that summer to record what was expected to be the makings of a single or two in a rudimentary studio – the band describe it as a shop front in Jamaica Plain, presumably similar to 'Record your band' joints like the one Frank Zappa had run in Cucamonga. In the event, none of the eight tracks we have are single length: 'Do You Believe in Magic?' is the shortest at 3:40, 'Good Day' the longest at 8:51. The band have also noted that they would have recorded other tracks from their repertoire such as 'Odyssee', except Dreyer thought them too long. But neither do they have the sense of a coherent album. In the event, somebody (and it's hard to imagine it was the band's decision) decided the acetates weren't good enough and the project was abandoned.

As outlined in the Collecting Nektar chapter at the end of this book, the session has been released officially three times: standalone as a fan-only set in 2008, and then on CD issues of *A Tab in the Ocean* in 2011 and *Remember the Future* in 2013. All the tracks, save 'Sealed With A Kiss', are Albrighton, Howden, Freeman, Moore originals.

The sound quality is very good, multi-tracked, and in stereo. We hear a competent progressive pop band, complete with organ swells and Kooper-style counterpoint. 'New Day Dawning' is a beautiful and mature reading, with some terrific three-part harmonies – and I sure do appreciate not being jarred out of the mood by the misogyny of 'Norwegian Wood', a song even more toxic than The Rolling Stones of the period. (They preyed on women too, but they didn't burn down their flats when their advances were spurned.) 'Do You Believe in Magic?' is the commercial gem, less rich on the harmonies, but shadowing Albrighton's verses deftly with reverb. His chunky fuzz solo is practically note-for-note the classic we know, building to a thundering barrage of chords.

The moodier 'Candlelight' had a less fêted future: it was only revisited in the studio once as part of a suite intended for *Sounds* during the first, largely fruitless session for that LP. Nevertheless, it's a storming proto-prog piece, slamming itself into the brick wall of an organ requiem. Churchy organ also introduces 'Good Day', coexisting awkwardly with its military drumming and Vanilla Fudge style chord changes. It's hard to imagine this as the future Nektar might have envisioned for themselves, somewhere in the same space as Deep Purple and Uriah Heep, but the stately pace and weighty guitar overdubs put it directly under the shadow of their pedestal. *Deep Purple in Rock* and the first Heep album ...*Very 'Eavy ...Very 'Umble* had both been released in June. Its highlight is a far too brief Wishbone Ash anticipating guitar duet in the closing seconds.

The rest is less engaging. 'The Life I've Been Leading' is fug-headed rock with its roots firmly in Moody Blues beat pop, though a jangly jazz centre with another of those sustain guitar duets does at least evoke glimpses of Spirit. The dreary 'Where Did You Go?' hangs on an incompetent tambourine rhythm, of all things, over which Freeman plays the most somnolent solo of his career. The song takes an eternity to rouse itself to a slow-burn guitar solo and Albrighton's pretty boy soul croon.

Hyland's 'Sealed with a Kiss' is pure perfection, so how could Nektar's members ever hope to make it their own? The answer was to Fudge it, literally: it's a slavish imitation of that band's ponderous minor key theatrics, right down to the monumental chorus harmonies over a guitar steal from The Beatles' 'You Never Give Me Your Money' – it gets old long before its four minutes are up. Finally, there's nothing about 'Our Love Will Last Forever' you couldn't surmise from the title.

Unidentified Flying Abstract

I'm going to be a stickler for accuracy here. Derek Moore's birthday is on 27 March. That day in 1974, a Wednesday, coincided with the wrap for basic sessions of *Down to Earth* at Chipping Norton Recording Studios. We know the band members celebrated both events with a jam session 'between the hours of 2:00 and 5:00 am.' Does that mean they were already in the studio overnight on the 26th, and toasted in the new day with the jam? Or is it more likely that, at the tail of the recording sessions on Moore's birthday, they let their hair down to celebrate and the jam was actually recorded on the early hours of the 28th?

This stuff is important to me, because the tape that resulted is a treasure. Three tracks – 'Oop's (Unidentified Flying Abstract)', 'Mundetango', and 'Summer Breeze' – with a measly run time of less than 16 minutes, were extracted the following year for release as the second side of *Sunday Night at London Roundhouse*, and a more satisfying 41 minutes as a standalone CD *Unidentified Flying Abstract* in 2002 meant to complement the release of the full *Sunday Night* concert. They have never been bundled together, though the same tape was regurgitated, in true Nektar fashion, for the third disc of Purple Pyramid's *Remember the Future* deluxe set in 2014. The pieces are all credited to Albrighton, Freeman, Howden, Moore (alphabetically in this case, regardless that 'Desolation Valley' had already been released), and we can assume that Brockett had no significant involvement.

To be honest, it's the release of an album like *Abstract*, even more than the first two studio LPs, that affords Nektar their dangerous musical schizophrenia. With a band like Hawkwind or Man, we can assume that no matter how technical the playing, they're always essentially space rock or psychedelia. With Pink Floyd, there's a clear division between the jamming and the prog periods. But *Abstract* seems anomalous, a stargazing excursion from a band that, lest we forget, was at that very moment attempting to bed their image in the elephant-urine stink of the sawdust of your mind. Maybe they needed to soar that night simply as an antidote to all this reality.

The tape, at least in the released sequence, kicks off with a lilting version of 'Desolation Valley' that skips through its changes apparently simply in the joy of playing a familiar piece since the band must have had no expectation of its release. Howden's economic fills and Moore's floating, disconnected phrases mesh with Freeman's organ drones, while Albrighton weaves clustered runs like saws with spiral blades.

'Oops' (here without its apostrophe) is a squabbling two-chord boogie with improvised words bleated powerfully by Albrighton as if they mean something – rock's primal trick. 'Mundetango' jokily merges the band's earnest driving rock with the bent-kneed stomp of a tango, exactly the same kind of perverse ethnological forgery that Can and Van der Graaf Generator delighted in – and like similar work by both those bands, by approximately halfway through it seems natural. There are more heartfelt mouth noises from Albrighton.

'One Mile Red' swanks and puffs like a rooster strutting up and down his five feet of rail. It's infectious slop thick enough to taste the undigested grit. 'The Ticket' morphs the rhythm to freeway rock blasted by sonic sunbeams. The embarrassed-sounding 'We Must Have Been Smashed' is actually rather special, jerking hesitantly forward like a game of sonic statues over which Albrighton plays meaty wah-wah.

The tape ends with 'Summer Breeze,' a brief guitar feature that the band played often but never recorded. Coincidentally, the earliest performance we know of was at the Roundhouse gig, whose vinyl it originally shared.

The Follies of Rupert Treacle

The jump cut in the centre of Nektar's career is fortuitous in a way, since it consigns prog's dark ages to a mere continuity glitch in the movie – skinny beards to florid paunches – rather than the endless years of musical stasis and regression that they actually were. True, it shifts us past days of reinvention and a few very bright spots indeed, but it also channels our attention away from acreages of dross.

Still, many of us lived those years, and endured them, and from this remove it's hard to see exactly what a man like Roye Albrighton did to keep his creative soul together between 1982 and 2000. There were few appearances, fewer songs. During his first hiatus from 1976–79, he'd helped form West

German pop fusion band Snowball (group image: the December page of a lonely farmers calendar), who released an album *Defroster* in 1978. Nektar fans most likely do not bother to put this in their ears even though it's actually fairly good. He then spent time in post-hit Quantum Jump, led by Rupert Hine, who also knew a thing or two about eyes on album covers. But in the long night, he did not play guitar for a big-hair outfit, shift into production, or sign up with Windham Hill. He certainly didn't embark upon a solo career. There was a failed pop band Grand Alliance in 1983, but that's about all.

Albrighton brought Nektar back together only when a near-fatal liver disease made him more amenable to picking up the baton. But in the midst of this crisis, he *did* put together a solo album. *The Follies of Rupert Treacle* was recorded at home in Stafford, England, in November and December 1998 and first released on Albrighton's own Treacle Records label the following year. My suspicion is that it was intended as a private gift to his own or friends' children, though the follies in question may well relate to the absurdity of creating it in the first place, all alone and with no hope of a smash. Voiceprint gave it a commercial issue in 2002, omitting a cover of Roy Orbison's 1964 song 'It's Over'. The only reason it's listed here is that Nektar also gave the Voiceprint version a release as the bonus disc for a 2020 CD of *Book of Days*, hence pulling it into the canon.

The album consists of sequences of electric guitar, some of them with synthesiser effects. Everything else is guitar synth driving Cubase's sampler modules. In 2004, Albrighton told *Progressive Ears* how it came about:

> Steve Hackett and I knew each other way back when Steve was leaving Genesis and I'd just left Nektar. He said he was working on this idea with the synthesiser guitar, which was in its early stages. I said that's funny because I'd just bought the first synthesiser guitar made by the Roland company. It was the GR-300, and Steve also had one. Later I heard Steve was on the road using the synthesiser guitar. Well, I was on the road as well, with a German band called Snowball, and was also playing synthesiser guitar. There was a bit of a parallel thing here, see. Anyway, I'd gone as far as I could with the synth guitar, and I took all the songs and put them on an album called *The Follies of Rupert Treacle*, and that's what it's all about.

There are two tracks with vocals, also layered by Albrighton alone, which apparently tell the story of the adventures and responsibilities of a child's imaginary friend. The kind of wimpy pixie, to judge from the cover, that any self-respecting kid would toss straight to the monsters under their bed.

'Sandman', the first of these songs, is lazy synth-pop with heavily dated percussion stabs and buzzy, undistinguished pads. It comes to life only when Albrighton's more familiar chunky guitar adds a solo in the closing minute. 'The Follies' is a fine Gilmour-style guitar workout over mid-tempo funk rock, while 'Rupert's Moon' has more in common with Manuel Göttsching, the album's most obvious jumping-off point.

On 'Pass the Fuzz', slurs of Fairlight-style bass joust with pan pipes to evoke overfed fairies bouncing maliciously on daisies. It's not the least bit trippy. The fuzz solo promised by the title is again the highlight, redeeming everything.

The other song, 'You're Not Alone' may be snooze pop, but it does provide a little conceptual continuity for those still struggling with the third chapter of this book. 'Hoping for the hand of the Lord to give you sight,' Albrighton sings, expressly linking the Nektar theme to the Christian redemption that was increasingly the preoccupation of his songs. The solo is much more majestic than the track deserves and sits oddly on top of all those pillowy sweeps.

'Treacle Star' steals the *Close Encounters of the Third Kind* motif to evoke the weighty themes of Floyd's *The Division Bell* – you'll long for Wright's Hammond to come surging in – while 'Dream' is chirpy pop with guitar where the vocals ought to be. On 'Rupert's Lament' (the title channelling King Crimson's 'Prince Rupert's Lament' on *Lizard*) Albrighton enlivens supermarket funk with the kind of clean guitar solo that would have transfixed little old ladies by the cucumber bin. Steve Hillage, I'll hazard, is the blueprint here.

With its surf sound effects, synth bird cheeps, and gamelan tones, 'Gabrielle's Bridge' is the album's attempt at contemporary ethnic ambient dub, though it's too poppy to evoke any kind of dreamtime. But the epic solos in 'The Stranger' bring us back gracefully to Gilmour. You guess what you're getting in the opening seconds, and you're not disappointed when you do.

Live Recordings

While we can assume that the major seams of Nektar's studio archive have been mined out, there's still the likelihood that the band are sitting on a respectable hoard of unreleased live music. In the liner notes to the *Live Anthology 1974–1976* box, Moore and Brockett claim, 'we have over 300 concerts to draw from.' I assume much of this is from the reformed band, but in context it does imply there's more of the golden age we have yet to hear. On *Door to the Future*, Brockett notes that he recorded 'many cassettes' for reference purposes. This list of notable official live releases is in chronological order of performance and becomes more selective as it progresses.

May 15, 1971: Ludwig-Georgs-Gymnasium, Darmstadt, West Germany

The earliest document of the band appears to be an NDR Television film of Nektar performing 'Good Day' in their youth club rehearsal space and looning about a snowy Darmstadt and frozen Hamburg in 1970, snippets of which were included in the 2002 NEARfest DVD. The earliest officially sanctioned live material is the fan-only 3CD set *Live in Darmstadt 1971* released in 2005 on the band's own Treacle Productions label, which contains seven minutes of what would become the 'Path of Light' section of *Remember the Future* (at the time known as 'We Are the Ocean') as one of its bonus tracks. It's dated 5 May, location unknown, but I think this is the correct date and venue.

November 13, 1971: Bessunger Turnhalle, Darmstadt, West Germany

This early hometown gig has been released across a plethora of bonus CDs, making it a chore to assimilate. The most complete reading is on *Live in Darmstadt 1971*, which was then used for the 3CD version of *Journey to the Centre of the Eye* released on Purple Pyramid in 2016. Both are all but impossible to find. In 2013, the gig was scattered as an 'official bootleg' over the bonus discs of three Purple Pyramid CD releases, carving up the performance to match the studio versions of the tracks: the *Journey* suite on *Journey*, 'Tab,' 'Porcelain Valley,' 'Cryin' in the Dark', and 'Desolation Valley' on *Tab*, and the rest on *...Sounds Like This*. In all released versions, some German announcements are missing, most notably a long introduction to *Journey*.

The full gig, in likely order, is: 'Good Day', 'Da-Da-Dum', 'A Tab in the Ocean', '1-2-3-4', 'Do You Believe in Magic?', a 47-minute rendition of the *Journey* suite, 'Cryin' in the Dark', 'Ron's On' (drum solo), 'Porcelain Valley', an improvisation labelled 'Daddy Jam', and 'New Day Dawning' complete with 'Norwegian Wood'. Even so early, as you can see, not just the next album but the one after were already in place, at least in embryo. You can understand why by 1973, Nektar wanted the *Sounds* material over and done with.

The recording is in a congested, shrill, and hissy mono recorded surreptitiously by an audience member or by a mike on a front-of-house mixing table. It doesn't matter with the band at such a peak and enjoying such an easy rapport with their audience. Even the technical issues are handled with good humour. 'We seem to have a hang-up on the lightshow,' Albrighton explains in English before what he hopes will be 'Tab'. 'The slides have fallen out!' The band perform a thunderous 'Da-Da-Dum' instead while Walters, presumably, scrambles to put them back in the correct order. He fails, leaving the band no choice but to take a break while they're being fixed.

The highlight is a squalling version of the *Journey* suite with improvised sections that delight in their mischievous clockwork, alternatively slamming the crowd into the floor and lofting it to the ceiling for eternities of heartbeat-inflected calm. Freeman's Caravan-style solos are particularly effective here and in 'Cryin' in the Dark', an oral sludge slapped across Albrighton's surgical guitar stabs and witch's brew cauldrons of wah-wah. The jam that climbs out of 'Porcelain Valley' is also notable, pushing hard against Moore's bass throb before flying apart into random guitar clatter like the shrapnel of exploded stars.

February 14, 1973: Palladium, Geneva, Switzerland

Regardless of the message sent by Nektar deciding to give the 2021 set *...Sounds Like Swiss* a cover image of the band posing next to a urinal, it's actually a terrific release. Geneva, the lesser of the two performances documented, is the most interesting because it's the only substantial golden age gig with footage. The hour-long studio performance in front of a small live audience was recorded by RTS and broadcast on *Kaléidospop* on 24 March the same year, though sadly, only a black and white tape remains. The *...Sounds Like Swiss* DVD presents it in full: the CD audio is identical save for clipping off an incomplete and sonically defective 'Da-Da-Dum.'

The sound is in rudimentary mono but listenable, and the band is at their ferocious peak. The highlights are a magnificent pulsing 'Squeeze' in which Albrighton's guitar (a solid-body) sandpapers the room, a coruscating mallet-driven 'Waves' which surely suggests some mutual inspiration with Man's 'The Storm', the muted-strings growl that drives Freeman's staccato '1-2-3-4' solos – this rendition is a career-high – and the runaway locomotive that screams headlong into 'King of Twilight'.

The main joy here, however, is to be able to see all four members performing. Since there's enough studio light to illuminate them, Brockett's lights (he's also visible manipulating them) are all but neutered. Freeman's key-slapping on the '1-2-3-4' introduction is a particular delight. But it is shag-haired beanpole Albrighton that compels throughout, in particular the intensity with which he belts out 'Good Day', proving he's as underrated a singer as he is prog's forgotten guitar hero. This footage ought to leave any unconvinced viewer mouth agape and utterly converted.

May 5, 1973: Palais De Beaulieu, Lausanne, Switzerland

The main event in ...*Sounds Like Swiss* is this 97-minute stereo soundboard from three months later, a period during which the band released ...*Sounds Like This* and began to piece together what would become *Remember the Future*. With this momentum behind them, *Journey* must have seemed positively prehistoric. Nevertheless, Nektar kick off with a daring spiral into the cosmic bowels of the suite – perhaps the acid peaked early on Hofmann's home soil – before shifting gears straight into 'Desolation Valley'. This dances daringly on the precipice of 'Waves' for what seems like hours before allowing itself the plunge into open air.

The banter is as informal as ever, with Albrighton wrongly assuming the next song will be 'Cast Your Fate' before Moore corrects him. 'Don't freak out, mate,' he retorts. In the event, 'A Day in the Life of a Preacher' is another great reading, Albrighton seeming to take genuine delight in his soul interjections, before a 'Squeeze' that channels Man's 'C'Mon' and a 'Mr. H' that is used as the vehicle for solos of furious intensity.

For many fans, the main event is likely to be a very early 'Let it Grow' but unfortunately, we don't know how it might have opened since the tape (which is a little fragmentary) fades in abruptly during what would become 'Recognition'. Its bulk is a breakneck funk workout. A chattery 'Odyssee' swerves the rhythm to jazz over which Albrighton and Moore do their best to unsettle the audience, but the triumphal 'Do You Believe in Magic?' guitar solo ensures the crowd leaves sated and high.

November 25, 1973: The Roundhouse, London, England

Capping their 1973 UK tour in support of ...*Sounds Like This*, Nektar's appearance as second billing to fast-fading Elephant's Memory at a Roundhouse festival was captured on 16-track tape by the Pye Records mobile in its entirety, but just 20 minutes were released on the *Sunday Night at London Roundhouse* LP released in May the following year. (For the rest of that release, see *Unidentified Flying Abstract* in the Other Studio Recordings chapter.) Those who hung around after Cockney Rebel (their first LP *The Human Menagerie* was released the same month) found a band still, incredibly, on the climb. As the band itself note in an onstage announcement, their breakthrough, *Remember the Future*, had been released in West Germany just two days before the show. But *Sunday Night* was never meant as more than a cash-in on the German success of *Remember*, and the unused tapes languished forgotten until a CD release of the full 105-minute set in 2002, this time with a definitive article. Needless to say, that is the version to get.

Historically, there are three highlights: a slow, achingly raw reading of 'Oh Willy' in the midst of an extraordinary near 20 minute 'A Day in the Life of a Preacher', the earliest released 'Summer Breeze', and the first almost complete rendition of *Remember*. Nektar perform the whole of the first side and a riotous 'Let it Grow', though not together.

It's a fine, immersive sound, beautifully separated across the channels, though for the first time the size of the venue leeches the occasion of its intimacy. The vocals, in particular, boom in a vast imagined space. It almost feels like Nektar have slipped out of our hands and are no longer our own. Still, you'll never do better sonically than the languid swells of 'Waves' or the smoke rings of echo on 'Squeeze'. Howden whips up an absolute froth of drums on 'Ron's On', there's an eternity of infectious dance rhythms in '1-2-3-4', and even at this early stage *Remember* is a marvel.

February 3, 1974: Stadthalle, Bietigheim, West Germany

The 2005 private CD release *Door to the Future: The Lightshow Tapes Volume 1 – German Tour 1974* extracted highlights from two of Brockett's cassettes, interweaving parts of this performance with Bielefeld on 12 June. The latter concert was released in full in 2019 on *Live Anthology 1974–1976*, leaving *Door* as the only place to hear more than 40 minutes from this gig.

It's worth the effort of tracking it down. The gig saw Nektar just about to decamp to England to record *Down to Earth*, and the historical highlights of the recording as we have it are versions of 'Fidgety Queen' and 'Show Me the Way' that are fully formed, save for a few lyric variations. The set also includes a brace of unrecorded, interwoven funk pieces, 'I Need Love' and 'Tomorrow', the latter one of those too-brief vocal spots for Freeman.

May 14, 1974: Stadthalle, Heidelberg, West Germany

Another of the bonus tracks on the 2005 set *Live in Darmstadt 1971* is a 15-minute rendition of the 'Cryin' in the Dark/King of Twilight' suite from this concert.

June 12, 1974: Rudolf-Oetker-Halle, Bielefeld, West Germany

Despite its unassuming size, the 5CD box *Live Anthology 1974–1976* is an excellent package, pulling together three separate performances from the band's peak. Fragments of this gig had previously appeared on *Door to The Future,* but here is almost the entire two-hour show (save for tape flips) in exemplary soundboard stereo, and it's crammed with highlights. Unlike the Roundhouse, the sound is tight, close, and shockingly visceral. You feel you're up there with the band, dancing the boards deliriously in the sheer pleasure of the event. It's the closest the majority of us will ever get to the thrill of the stage – certainly to the privilege of an on-form band enjoying every moment of their success in front of a hall full of fans. This is *the* Nektar concert to revere.

It kicks off monumentally with the first half of *Remember*. You'll have to wait the entire gig for the encore's second half. But sandwiching the band's past into the masterwork is an intuitive choice. So much of early Nektar evolved from a single continuity of creative energy and this is almost our last chance to enjoy these four men propelling each other forward all by themselves. *Down to Earth* added brass, and *Recycled* synths and choir. Bielefeld catalogues, succinctly and as if for the ages, everything the core band achieved.

Still, what's notable is the material that has already been left behind in less than five years of writing and touring. There's no *Journey* at all, and no 'Tab', nor do the band play '1-2-3-4', 'Do You Believe In Magic?', or 'Odyssee'. Bielefeld is as much a future. As well as a host of *Earth* material to integrate, it also begins to incorporate Freeman's electronics. It hints at the opening of extraordinary new horizons.

Musically, the gig is as good as it gets. Moore's clear tone and adventurous phrasing are particularly notable. 'Squeeze' is spry and beguiling, while 'Cryin' in the Dark' reveals the band's rock engine at its punishing pinnacle. Vocally, Albrighton evinces understandable fatigue at the tail of a long European tour, but his voice's cracked weariness suits the material and actually benefits the more emotional material like 'Show Me the Way'.

Of the lesser-known music, 'Anyway/Sorrow' is an unadorned three-voice ballad sung merely to Albrighton's guitar. It's heartbreakingly beautiful, making me wish the band had found a space for it on an album – the highlight, perhaps, of the disc to follow *Recycled*. Surely slated for that disc, too, would have been 'The Devil's Door', which only found itself canon when the opening of this performance was used for a new rendition of the song on *The Other Side*. There's also a cathartic outing for one of the seldom-played centrepieces from *Earth*, 'Little Boy', and the only known stage rendition of 'Nelly the Elephant' in the golden age. It's a fuzz-splattered hoot.

September 28, 1974: Academy Of Music, New York, NY, USA

This memento of the band's barnstorming first tour of the US, fortuitously captured by prog-focused WNEW-FM, was, for years, the only substantial live record of the band available to purchase since it was released over two double LPs – *Live in New York* (1977) and *More Live in New York* (1978) – which used a dummy head during mixing to try to place you virtually in the venue. A butchered version of the former and a straight transcription of the latter both made it to CD in 1991. The full two-hour show finally received a 5.1 channel SACD release in 2004. For reasons best known to itself, Purple Pyramid then placed 72 minutes of the concert on the bonus disc of a 2014 CD release of *Remember the Future*.

The sound is flatter and less engaging than Bielefeld, but here the gig is all about the spectacle, as imagined through the eyes of a wildly appreciative audience, and the palpable sense of relief that the band had finally broken big. We're treated to yet more new material: a suite comprising 'Marvellous Moses' (which Moore introduces as a 'special song' the band wrote for the US) and 'It's All Over' almost a year before the recording of *Recycled* and 15 months from its US release. This is also the first released gig where the band let their substantial hair down for a rock'n'roll rave-up in the encore.

April 26, 1975: Palace Theatre, Detroit, IL, USA

Just before recording *Recycled*, Nektar used a spring US tour to hone the music they would include on the disc. The earliest released side one suite was performed here, though the band admit it still doesn't have a title. It's nevertheless a near-complete 17-minute reading, performed with all the breakneck propulsion of the album – of course, it lacks the Larry Fast sequences – and with much of its lyric in place. There's also a song that didn't make the disc, an attractive ballad called 'Look Just Once More', which was likely considered too close to 'It's All Over'.

The gig, immortalised on an uncomfortably strident stereo tape, was first issued incomplete as a Collector's Corner set called *Live in Detroit 1975* in 2008, and was then included in full (the longest to date at 131 minutes) on *Live Anthology 1974–1976*. The '1-2-3-4' jam covers extensive aural ground, the 'Let It Grow' apocalypse is suitably all-flattening, and Albrighton's dental surgery during 'Oh Willy' is particularly gruesome.

May 3, 1975: Academy Of Music, New York, NY, USA

Two hours of this gig were released as a fan-only download in 2020 called *Live Again in New York*. Almost identical to the Detroit show above.

September 12, 1976: Night Gallery, Waukegan, IL, USA

The last of the shows in *Live Anthology 1974–1976* is one disc only of the third night in a snowbound club in which, the way the box tells it, both Nektar and their audience were held captive by the bad weather and the band had devolved to stoned jamming. That seems a little unfair. The one unparented improvisation here, unnecessarily labelled 'Epiphonic Vomit Jam', is anything but repugnant, however mucilaginous the wah-wah and electronic effects on Albrighton's Epiphone. Over its 13 minutes, it traverses landscapes of real charm, particularly when Freeman drives the truck. The majority of the 80-minute tape consists of the standard set played beautifully.

Circumstances aside, Waukegan is a suitable place to end our substantial documents of the original band since the small venue meant a closely focused soundboard and performers who seemed to have turned full circle back to their Darmstadt days. We may be in a different continent, but the ambience is identical, a band contracted to an island of warmth and connection in the big chill – and, to complete the regression still more, like a film running callously backwards, a guitarist who was about to step away from the other three leaving a clutch of great songs in their hands.

December 12, 1976: County College Of Morris, Randolph, NJ, USA

But that wasn't *quite* the end. The final bonus tracks from *Live in Darmstadt 1971* are 17 minutes of fragments from this gig, consisting of 'Summer

Breeze', 'The Dream Nebula', and 'Let it Grow', missives spit across the ether from days before Albrighton quit.

October 8, 1977: Hofstra University, Hempstead, NY, USA

Our single live record of the Dave Nelson band is this mediocre FM broadcast long labelled 18 October in tape-sharing circles. My best guess is the date above. 'Midnite Lite' was released on the 2005 CD of *Magic is a Child*, and a full disc's worth of the concert on the 2014 reissue.

We're lucky to have it, given that at the time, WLIR was transitioning away from prog to new wave and synth pop, and indeed the days when a band like Nektar could command a 73-minute feature were fast fading. But the band's own change of focus is also clear: of the 11 tracks released, seven are from *Magic is a Child* – and of course, the band would want to promote this – and none of the four old standards are played with much in the way of extemporisation – 'King of Twilight' is the most extensive at 12 minutes. The *Remember* and *Recycled* suites are each dispatched at around the ten-minute mark, the former a sort of hits reel of the poppier parts that segues straight out of 'Train From Nowhere', the latter unfortunately making it clear that Nelson doesn't have an ounce of Albrighton's vocal power. The 'Oh Willy'/'Mr. H' suite played standalone gets almost nine encouraging minutes, but it's too little to satisfy.

Still, the crowd seems fully onboard. When Nelson mentions the new album, an audience member shouts, 'it's great!', a reaction that for sure must have given the band unwarranted hope.

June 29, 2002: Patriots Theater, Trenton, NJ, USA

We skip ahead a quarter century to pick up Nektar again with the surprise announcement that the original four, plus Brockett, had agreed to reunite for NEARfest 2002. The band headlined the first day of the event over Isildurs Bane and Miriodor, both at the vanguard of a brilliantly eclectic new generation of prog bands. The old guard was the draw, though, as it remains to this day: the festival culminated the following night with sets by Caravan and Steve Hackett.

But Nektar was the story, and an event of such importance was documented voraciously on a 90-minute DVD rushed into stores by Classic Rock Productions as *Live,* too fast to bother with a worthwhile cover design. A matching CD set, *Greatest Hits Live,* added the sequences omitted from the film: 'A Day in the Life of a Preacher' and most of *Remember the Future.* Be warned that the footage has been repackaged under different names since, including as a bundle with Gong and Hawkwind called *Acid Rock* in 2004.

Albrighton detailed the circumstances of the band's reunion to *Guitar International* in 2011:

> We were approached by the NEARfest organisation to do a show with the original line-up. We all practised the music at home alone and then met up

at our sound engineer's rehearsal studios for a run-through of the show. It was fun to see the guys again. Of course, there were difficult moments there, but we had five days [of] rehearsals before the show and eventually, it all came together.

A set was agreed, drawing mostly from the classic material along with scant concessions to *Man in the Moon* and *The Prodigal Son*: nothing from *Journey*, the whole of *Tab*, 'Preacher' alone from ...*Sounds Like This* to signify that album's near total denigration (no 'Good Day', 'Do You Believe in Magic?', '1-2-3-4', or 'Odyssee'), the whole of *Remember* apparently for the first time ever (but as usual not in one block), 'Nelly the Elephant' and 'Fidgety Queen' from *Down to Earth*, and the first side suite along with 'It's All Over' from *Recycled*.

The band perform enthusiastically, and the DVD's blend of contemporary and vintage footage, most particularly from *The Old Grey Whistle Test*, works well. Larry Fast brings his synths along, though – for the most part – they're pad washes. He is featured playing the 'Nelly' melody and, of course, in *Recycled*. The sound's thickened further by vocals from Michelle Eckert and Maureen McIntyre, and by percussionist Scott Krentz, for all three of whom this would seem to have been a career peak since it's basically the only rock credit they ever got. Krentz commands a spotlight throughout, all but wrecking Brockett's slides, but there's fun to be had watching Albrighton move in and out of the beam. When he heads over to engage in rock star poses with Moore, that might not be as familial as it seems.

Were Nektar rejuvenated? Not really. They didn't return to the studio despite the hope the band expressed in the DVD's interviews that they would do a new album. There was a brief roll across the world, following NEARfest with a second festival at the same venue in October (also featuring Asia, Focus, and Uriah Heep) and a handful of shows in the US, UK, and Germany in the summer of 2003 – eight appearances by the reformed band in total – before Moore bailed. Albrighton and Howden kept the Nektar continuity alive for more than a decade, but the homecoming show in Darmstadt on 20 July was the last time the originals ever shared the boards together.

March 12, 2005: Harmonie, Bonn, Germany

The tours that followed the *Evolution* album – by a band consisting of Albrighton, Howden, bassist Randy Dembo, and keyboard player Tom Hughes – have been fairly well documented, with official releases including the fan club issues *2004 Tour Live* (which spins together tracks from Arlington, Atlanta, and Milwaukee with two anachronistic excerpts from Dortmund on March 11, 2005), *Live in Germany 2005* (the complete Dortmund show), and two bonus tracks on the 2008 version of *The Boston Tapes*. But the highlight of this period was another filmed performance, in this case for the *Rockpalast* Crossroads Festival in Bonn, alongside Robin Trower and the John Butler Trio.

What resulted was a fine two-DVD set called *Pure*, with a host of bonus material, including a more intimate show featuring Albrighton on acoustic guitar recorded a day later. The main set has solidified around its classics: complete performances of the *Tab* and *Remember* albums (the latter, finally, as one block, the highlight here), the first side of *Recycled*, and selections from ...*Sounds Like This* ('Good Day', 'Cast Your Fate', 'A Day In The Life Of A Preacher') and *Down to Earth* ('That's Life', 'Fidgety Queen', 'Show Me the Way'). There's only the merest smattering of newer material.

The lack of a darkened room lightshow seems far from a handicap, revealing a simpler, more connective band, and Albrighton leads with surety and genuine warmth. The abrasion may have been worn away by time, but when the band decides to rock – for example, on 'Mr. H' – it can still shred the room.

November 10, 2005: Teatro Municipal, Niterói, Brazil

The 2011 CD release of *Remember the Future* on the ItsAboutMusic label included well over an hour and a half of this gig (dated incorrectly to 2007), including the entire *Remember* suite. For sure, it's best savoured for its occasion, but the sound is exemplary and the Albrighton-Howden-Dembo-Hughes band scorches through the material, with a particularly muscular suite again the standout.

Fortyfied

The band continued to convulse, replacing both bassist and keyboard player in 2006 and again in 2007. By the end of that year, Albrighton and Howden had settled – at least for a few years – on Peter Pichl and Klaus Henatsch, the latter to become a fixture up until the end of Albrighton's life and lead the 'New Nektar' formation in 2018. But the studio album *Book of Days* featured the previous incarnation. Therefore, in 2009 the group's private Treacle Music label issued the humorously-titled live set *Fortyfied* in order 'to alleviate any misconceptions as to how strong the band still are', according to Albrighton in an interview with *It's Psychedelic Baby* in 2012. The aim seemed to be to create a calling card to the US, perhaps even a demonstration directed at potential bookers and promoters in advance of the band's May tour that Nektar were fighting fit.

The recordings, assembled from a 2008 tour of Germany, did indeed form the ideal introduction, hitting all the highs from a long career. There's a nod to *Journey* ('The Dream Nebula'), the whole of *Tab*, sections of *Remember the Future* (the second half) and *Recycled* (the first half), alongside selections from ...*Sounds Like This* ('A Day in the Life of a Preacher'), *Man in the Moon* (the title track), and *Evolution* ('The Debate'). There are even three tracks from *Book of Days*. This time around, only *Down to Earth*, *Magic is a Child*, and *The Prodigal Son* are omitted, and one of these is no surprise at all. But whatever its aims, the US tour was short.

September 3, 2011: Key Club, West Hollywood, CA, USA

With Pichl replaced by Lux Vibratus, the band embarked on another US tour in August 2011, playing a few dates with suitably chemicalised Huw Lloyd-Langton and totally wigged-out Brainticket. The jaunt was commemorated with filmed performances by all three performers here on the last night, released as a DVD set *Space Rock Invasion* the following year. Nektar's 90 minutes were issued separately as a two CD/DVD pack in 2021 under the same title.

Rather than grumpy old men in disreputable company, there's actually something fitting about Nektar immersed in fractals and lava lamp globs in a Sunset Strip club for roughly 200 patrons whose acid hadn't yet worn off. Albrighton is endearingly informal, bantering with the audience and geeing up his own exhausted troops. It wasn't the end – his final shows in 2015 were documented on a 2016 solo release *Up Close* and a 2017 Nektar CD called *Live in Bremen* – and it may not be the current paradigm of the band or the ideal starting point for the uncommitted, but it's not a bad way to be remembered.

March 7, 2020: The Wildey Theatre, Edwardsville, IL, USA

Moore and Howden plunged on, commencing an encouragingly robust touring schedule that continues to this day. As evidence of the road ahead, the download-only audio and video set *Live from The Wildey Theatre* captures a moment just before lockdown and with another decade to celebrate under the band's belt. To extraordinary visuals from Mick Brockett are meshed the familiar and not-so-familiar: there's a rendition of 'It's All in the Mind' from *Journey* and almost the entire *The Other Side*. The release finds Nektar poised perfectly between prog's musical dexterity and psychedelia's abandon, a sweet spot that the band have now pretty much staked for their own.

Collecting Nektar

This chapter explores entry points into the band, the state of their current catalogue, and what we might hope for in the future.

Single and multi-artist compilations

These days, the ability to preview just about any music you're interested in for free online means that single-artist compilations aimed at the curious are largely irrelevant. And clearly, there's an established gateway into Nektar, consisting of *Remember the Future,* which is an album even the uncommitted should own, and *Recycled* once you've assimilated that.

Given that those two albums are best experienced in full, the golden age will always be a difficult period to compile on silver disc, let alone LP. New listeners may be best off with Bellaphon's *5 Essential Albums* CD set released in 2019. It gives you no frills, no bonus track editions of the studio releases from *Tab* to *Recycled* – *Journey,* curiously, is omitted.

If you really prefer extracts to full conceptual works, there are a few options. The earliest compilation, simply called *Nektar* (1976), covers only the first three albums but is notable for its iconic bee cover. Neither *Thru the Ears* nor *Best of Nektar* (both 1978) are worth seeking out. The first attempt at a CD retrospective *The Dream Nebula* (1998) is a little more comprehensive, but my recommendation is the 2-CD box *Retrospektive 1969–1980* (2011), which is interesting because it includes two A-sides by Rainbows. The rest, as the title suggests, comprises album excerpts up to *Man in the Moon.* They're not the tracks I would have chosen, but good enough.

All these releases cover only the golden age. There has never been a compilation of the reformed band's work. What would a *whole career* overview even look like, were there no licensing issues to prevent it? For this, we'd have to get brutal, ditching entire albums in order to drill down to the most attractive introduction we can. Confining ourselves only to material released on original studio albums (nothing live, nothing from the bonus tracks) – here's a tentative suggestion:

1. A Better Way (*Time Machine*) 9:17
2. Over Krakatoa (*Book of Days*) 5:06
3. Listen (*Magic is a Child*) 6:02
4. Odyssee (*...Sounds Like This*) 14:37
5. Show Me the Way (*Down to Earth*) 5:55
6. Drifting (*The Other Side*) 9:12
7. Always (*Evolution*) 7:04
8. A Tab in the Ocean (*A Tab in the Ocean*) 16:39
9. It's All Over (*Recycled*) 5:22

The compilation runs 1:19:05 and the only editing you need do is trim 'It's All Over' to a cold open on its first chord.

There are no surprises here, no left-field deep-dive revisions, simply a means to introduce the full breadth of an important band on one CD to modern ears that need to be impressed from first note to last. Purposefully, it's not in chronological order and it includes nothing from *Remember*. Stick it as a giveaway to the cover of a physical classic rock magazine (do those things still exist?) and watch the fans roll in. But of course, it's just a suggestion, and your ideal Nektar disc isn't going to look like that – nor would mine, for that matter.

In contrast to single-artist compilations, multi-artist compilations are vitally important if they're intelligently curated, introducing listeners to lesser-known bands all in a similar style. Currently, Cherry Red Records leads the way, in particular David Wells's Grapefruit imprint, but they have not yet attempted anything that might incorporate Nektar.

The band have appeared on quite a few multi-artist compilations, however, sometimes in bizarre company. For example, the 1974 LP *Various: 20 Super Pop Hits* listed 'Fidgety Queen' alongside work by the likes of Leonard Cohen, Cat Stevens, and The Tremeloes. Prog fans may be attracted to the huge 1996 *Supernatural Fairy Tales* CD box by Rhino, and not just for Nektar's 'Questions and Answers'. Psychedelic fans will find the band on *The Psychedelic Journey* (2012), which placed 'Astronaut's Nightmare' alongside Brainticket, Gong, Guru Guru, Hawkwind, and Tangerine Dream. The same track also made it onto 2016's *Space Rock: An Interstellar Traveler's Guide*.

For Nektar's contribution to *Who Are You: An All Star Tribute to The Who*, see the *A Spoonful Of Time* chapter.

And then there's Iron Maiden, the only A-lister to have covered the band's songs. You'll find Maiden's rendition of 'King of Twilight' (incorporating 'Cryin' in the Dark') on the B-side of the 1984 single 'Aces High' and on some extended versions of *Powerslave*.

Live recordings

At the very least, fans of the golden age need the complete *Sunday Night at the London Roundhouse* and *Live in New York* CDs, plus *Live Anthology 1974– 1976* (there's no overlap) and *...Sounds Like Swiss*. As you'd expect, there's a great deal more audio of the reformed band.

Surprisingly little bootleg (audience-recorded) material circulates from the golden age, at least in comparison with other bands of the same vintage such as Pink Floyd. With the material listed above and the possibility of much more in the vault, it's not something most listeners will need to seek out. We should expect further Nektar recordings to be released as and when the band deem it financially viable.

What we probably shouldn't hold out hope for is much in the way of period visuals. For a band whose major selling point in the 1970s was their lightshow, we have almost no evidence on which to gauge its power. There appears to be no substantial extant live footage of the band during the golden age whatsoever.

There's also scant TV studio footage, save a black and white live concert performance from 1973 included in ...*Sounds Like Swiss*. A brief colour set on *The Old Grey Whistle Test* in 1973 gives us 'Desolation Valley' and 'Waves' without the lightshow, substituting an annoying camera overlay. This is a mixed blessing, since it does enable us to concentrate on Albrighton's Epiphone semi-acoustic guitar skills and Freeman's Wright-like organ playing. There's also a very short excerpt of the band miming to *Remember the Future* on German TV the following year, possibly again with overlay. There might have been more, except that Nektar refused to perform on TV because they weren't allowed to perform with their lights. Both of the above snippets were included in the NEARfest DVD.

Multichannel mixes

Nektar recorded several of their early albums with quadraphonic in mind, but no pure quadraphonic mix has ever been available on optical disc. The band's 5.1 remixes, listed in the body of this book, use the quad as their base, adding upmixed centre and bass channels, but were all issued only on SACD. It's rapidly becoming obsolete technology, risking discs that no longer have the hardware to play them.

Still, Eclectic Discs founder Mark Powell, the engineer on those remixes, holds out hope for an update. Regarding the omission of some of the key albums on 5.1, he told *Sound & Vision* in 2020:

> The [*Tab*] multitracks did exist, but we decided not to do it probably because of the budget at the time. But it's something I'd like to go back to again. I'd like to go back to *Recycled* as well, but I have a funny feeling some of the multitracks are missing on that one. ...*Sounds Like This* did have the 16-track masters there, and there was a version that appeared for about five minutes, but we had to change gears because we had to close down the old label for various reasons, and then set up Esoteric Recordings instead. We've been talking about getting access to the Nektar catalogue and doing new 5.1 versions of things properly – revisiting it all, and getting the catalogue out there again.

Reissues

Labels like Eclectic Discs (which published the Dream Nebula imprint for the band) have not been the most careful curators according to Albrighton, who expressed frustration at the way the band's legacy had been handled. In 2011 he told *Aural Innovations*:

> There's a company called Eclectic Discs which got the rights to release the albums, but unfortunately, they released the albums not exactly as we wanted. They were only supposed to release exactly the album that came out originally. They put all kinds of [bonus] stuff on there. Which some

people think is great, but we didn't approve it. So Bellaphon pulled it and it went a little bit dead for a while. And then I went to see Bellaphon Records and said we need to get some product out there. Even if we never make another album, there's still Nektar material from the past. And they said okay, and this then led to licensing out to ItsAboutMusic and, of course, Cleopatra. We collected live material from previous tours to release special editions together with the real albums. They're completely different.

What they were, in fact, was worse. Nektar fans must traverse a minefield of releases from labels such as Cleopatra's Purple Pyramid imprint that endlessly regurgitate existing content. For example, the 2013 CD of *Journey to the Centre of the Eye* included a second disc of live material from Darmstadt in 1971. So did the 2013 CDs of *A Tab in the Ocean* and *...Sounds Like This,* along with the 2016 CD of *Journey*. Fan club releases such as Nektar's 'Collector's Corner' strand have also been released on reissues. The 2008 Collector's Corner release of *The Boston Tapes* was followed by their release as *In the Beginning – The Boston Tapes* on a 2011 CD of *Tab* and *The 1970 Boston Tapes* on a 2013 CD of *Remember the Future.*

Right now, the Nektar completist has no choice but to wade through all the different releases. By definition, it means you're going to buy Nektar on CD. Those who want Nektar on vinyl have fewer choices and an easier purchase route but be warned that several of the more recent albums have never been released on LP.

Box sets

As I write, Nektar are one of the few bands of their stature never to have warranted a career box set. True, they have mustered a succession of 'deluxe' editions, generally two or three CD sets. There have been small-format boxes of studio and live work, but no attempt to place the band on the big shelf: multiple discs slotted into a sumptuous book and enlivened with memorabilia of the kind that Caravan, Gentle Giant, and Van der Graaf Generator have enjoyed recently. Are the numbers simply not there?

Nektar may never command a reissue campaign as jaw-droppingly lavish as King Crimson's or as fan-pleasing as Jethro Tull's, but you'd expect a little more care than regular revamping of the same-old albums with the same-old liner notes.

We'd buy all this stuff *one last time* in a definitive box, with Blu-ray multichannel mixes and all the extant live recordings, curated with love and presented as a lavish gift to long-suffering fans. We'd buy it because it consigns the headache of all the previous reissues to the bin. We'd buy it because it gives us something to cherish and a signifier of our regard for the band. And we'd buy it because Nektar are worth it, as I hope this book has demonstrated.

Future studio albums

All things willing, this isn't the end of the band's studio career. Nektar continue to tour post-lockdown, and Moore told *Progressive Rock Journal* in 2021 that new material was on the way:

> We are currently writing new stuff for a new album. This will also include music that was left over from 1978 with a 2022 spin on it.

With luck, it will be in the stores by the time you read this.

Also available from Sonicbond

On Track series
Allman Brothers Band – Andrew Wild 978-1-78952-252-5
Tori Amos – Lisa Torem 978-1-78952-142-9
Asia – Peter Braidis 978-1-78952-099-6
Badfinger – Robert Day-Webb 978-1-878952-176-4
Barclay James Harvest – Keith and Monica Domone 978-1-78952-067-5
The Beatles – Andrew Wild 978-1-78952-009-5
The Beatles Solo 1969-1980 – Andrew Wild 978-1-78952-030-9
Blue Oyster Cult – Jacob Holm-Lupo 978-1-78952-007-1
Blur – Matt Bishop 978-178952-164-1
Marc Bolan and T.Rex – Peter Gallagher 978-1-78952-124-5
Kate Bush – Bill Thomas 978-1-78952-097-2
Camel – Hamish Kuzminski 978-1-78952-040-8
Captain Beefheart – Opher Goodwin 978-1-78952-235-8
Caravan – Andy Boot 978-1-78952-127-6
Cardiacs – Eric Benac 978-1-78952-131-3
Nick Cave and The Bad Seeds – Dominic Sanderson 978-1-78952-240-2
Eric Clapton Solo – Andrew Wild 978-1-78952-141-2
The Clash – Nick Assirati 978-1-78952-077-4
Crosby, Stills and Nash – Andrew Wild 978-1-78952-039-2
Creedence Clearwater Revival – Tony Thompson 978-178952-237-2
The Damned – Morgan Brown 978-1-78952-136-8
Deep Purple and Rainbow 1968-79 – Steve Pilkington 978-1-78952-002-6
Dire Straits – Andrew Wild 978-1-78952-044-6
The Doors – Tony Thompson 978-1-78952-137-5
Dream Theater – Jordan Blum 978-1-78952-050-7
Eagles – John Van der Kiste 978-1-78952-260-0
Electric Light Orchestra – Barry Delve 978-1-78952-152-8
Elvis Costello and The Attractions – Georg Purvis 978-1-78952-129-0
Emerson Lake and Palmer – Mike Goode 978-1-78952-000-2
Fairport Convention – Kevan Furbank 978-1-78952-051-4
Peter Gabriel – Graeme Scarfe 978-1-78952-138-2
Genesis – Stuart MacFarlane 978-1-78952-005-7
Gentle Giant – Gary Steel 978-1-78952-058-3
Gong – Kevan Furbank 978-1-78952-082-8
Hall and Oates – Ian Abrahams 978-1-78952-167-2
Hawkwind – Duncan Harris 978-1-78952-052-1
Peter Hammill – Richard Rees Jones 978-1-78952-163-4
Roy Harper – Opher Goodwin 978-1-78952-130-6
Jimi Hendrix – Emma Stott 978-1-78952-175-7
The Hollies – Andrew Darlington 978-1-78952-159-7
The Human League and The Sheffield Scene – Andrew Darlington 978-1-78952-186-3
Iron Maiden – Steve Pilkington 978-1-78952-061-3
Jefferson Airplane – Richard Butterworth 978-1-78952-143-6
Jethro Tull – Jordan Blum 978-1-78952-016-3
Elton John in the 1970s – Peter Kearns 978-1-78952-034-7
The Incredible String Band – Tim Moon 978-1-78952-107-8
Iron Maiden – Steve Pilkington 978-1-78952-061-3
Joe Jackson – Richard James 978-1-78952-189-4
Billy Joel – Lisa Torem 978-1-78952-183-2
Judas Priest – John Tucker 978-1-78952-018-7
Kansas – Kevin Cummings 978-1-78952-057-6
The Kinks – Martin Hutchinson 978-1-78952-172-6
Korn – Matt Karpe 978-1-78952-153-5
Led Zeppelin – Steve Pilkington 978-1-78952-151-1

Level 42 – Matt Philips 978-1-78952-102-3
Little Feat – Georg Purvis - 978-1-78952-168-9
Aimee Mann – Jez Rowden 978-1-78952-036-1
Joni Mitchell – Peter Kearns 978-1-78952-081-1
The Moody Blues – Geoffrey Feakes 978-1-78952-042-2
Motorhead – Duncan Harris 978-1-78952-173-3
Nektar – Scott Meze – 978-1-78952-257-0
New Order – Dennis Remmer – 979-1-78952-249-5
Laura Nyro – Philip Ward 978-1-78952-182-5
Mike Oldfield – Ryan Yard 978-1-78952-060-6
Opeth – Jordan Blum 978-1-78-952-166-5
Pearl Jam – Ben L. Connor 978-1-78952-188-7
Tom Petty – Richard James 978-1-78952-128-3
Pink Floyd – 978-1-78952-242-6 Richard Butterworth
Porcupine Tree – Nick Holmes 978-1-78952-144-3
Queen – Andrew Wild 978-1-78952-003-3
Radiohead – William Allen 978-1-78952-149-8
Rancid – Paul Matts 989-1-78952-187-0
Renaissance – David Detmer 978-1-78952-062-0
The Rolling Stones 1963-80 – Steve Pilkington 978-1-78952-017-0
The Smiths and Morrissey – Tommy Gunnarsson 978-1-78952-140-5
Spirit – Rev. Keith A. Gordon – 978-1-78952- 248-8
Stackridge – Alan Draper 978-1-78952-232-7
Status Quo the Frantic Four Years – Richard James 978-1-78952-160-3
Steely Dan – Jez Rowden 978-1-78952-043-9
Steve Hackett – Geoffrey Feakes 978-1-78952-098-9
Tears For Fears – Paul Clark - 978-178952-238-9
Thin Lizzy – Graeme Stroud 978-1-78952-064-4
Tool – Matt Karpe 978-1-78952-234-1
Toto – Jacob Holm-Lupo 978-1-78952-019-4
U2 – Eoghan Lyng 978-1-78952-078-1
UFO – Richard James 978-1-78952-073-6
Van Der Graaf Generator – Dan Coffey 978-1-78952-031-6
Van Halen – Morgan Brown – 9781-78952-256-3
The Who – Geoffrey Feakes 978-1-78952-076-7
Roy Wood and the Move – James R Turner 978-1-78952-008-8
Yes – Stephen Lambe 978-1-78952-001-9
Frank Zappa 1966 to 1979 – Eric Benac 978-1-78952-033-0
Warren Zevon – Peter Gallagher 978-1-78952-170-2
10CC – Peter Kearns 978-1-78952-054-5

Decades Series
The Bee Gees in the 1960s – Andrew Mon Hughes et al 978-1-78952-148-1
The Bee Gees in the 1970s – Andrew Mon Hughes et al 978-1-78952-179-5
Black Sabbath in the 1970s – Chris Sutton 978-1-78952-171-9
Britpop – Peter Richard Adams and Matt Pooler 978-1-78952-169-6
Phil Collins in the 1980s – Andrew Wild 978-1-78952-185-6
Alice Cooper in the 1970s – Chris Sutton 978-1-78952-104-7
Curved Air in the 1970s – Laura Shenton 978-1-78952-069-9
Donovan in the 1960s – Jeff Fitzgerald 978-1-78952-233-4
Bob Dylan in the 1980s – Don Klees 978-1-78952-157-3
Brian Eno in the 1970s – Gary Parsons 978-1-78952-239-6
Faith No More in the 1990s – Matt Karpe 978-1-78952-250-1
Fleetwood Mac in the 1970s – Andrew Wild 978-1-78952-105-4
Fleetwood Mac in the 1980s – Don Klees 978-178952-254-9

Focus in the 1970s – Stephen Lambe 978-1-78952-079-8
Free and Bad Company in the 1970s – John Van der Kiste 978-1-78952-178-8
Genesis in the 1970s – Bill Thomas 978178952-146-7
George Harrison in the 1970s – Eoghan Lyng 978-1-78952-174-0
Kiss in the 1970s – Peter Gallagher 978-1-78952-246-4
Manfred Mann's Earth Band in the 1970s – John Van der Kiste 978178952-243-3
Marillion in the 1980s – Nathaniel Webb 978-1-78952-065-1
Van Morrison in the 1970s – Peter Childs - 978-1-78952-241-9
Mott the Hoople and Ian Hunter in the 1970s – John Van der Kiste 978-1-78-952-162-7
Pink Floyd In The 1970s – Georg Purvis 978-1-78952-072-9
Suzi Quatro in the 1970s – Darren Johnson 978-1-78952-236-5
Roxy Music in the 1970s – Dave Thompson 978-1-78952-180-1
Status Quo in the 1980s – Greg Harper 978-1-78952-244-0
Tangerine Dream in the 1970s – Stephen Palmer 978-1-78952-161-0
The Sweet in the 1970s – Darren Johnson 978-1-78952-139-9
Uriah Heep in the 1970s – Steve Pilkington 978-1-78952-103-0
Van der Graaf Generator in the 1970s – Steve Pilkington 978-1-78952-245-7
Yes in the 1980s – Stephen Lambe with David Watkinson 978-1-78952-125-2

On Screen series
Carry On... – Stephen Lambe 978-1-78952-004-0
David Cronenberg – Patrick Chapman 978-1-78952-071-2
Doctor Who: The David Tennant Years – Jamie Hailstone 978-1-78952-066-8
James Bond – Andrew Wild 978-1-78952-010-1
Monty Python – Steve Pilkington 978-1-78952-047-7
Seinfeld Seasons 1 to 5 – Stephen Lambe 978-1-78952-012-5

Other Books
1967: A Year In Psychedelic Rock 978-1-78952-155-9
1970: A Year In Rock – John Van der Kiste 978-1-78952-147-4
1973: The Golden Year of Progressive Rock 978-1-78952-165-8
Babysitting A Band On The Rocks – G.D. Praetorius 978-1-78952-106-1
Eric Clapton Sessions – Andrew Wild 978-1-78952-177-1
Derek Taylor: For Your Radioactive Children – Andrew Darlington 978-1-78952-038-5
The Golden Road: The Recording History of The Grateful Dead – John Kilbride 978-1-78952-156-6
Iggy and The Stooges On Stage 1967-1974 – Per Nilsen 978-1-78952-101-6
Jon Anderson and the Warriors – the road to Yes – David Watkinson 978-1-78952-059-0
Misty: The Music of Johnny Mathis – Jakob Baekgaard 978-1-78952-247-1
Nu Metal: A Definitive Guide – Matt Karpe 978-1-78952-063-7
Tommy Bolin: In and Out of Deep Purple – Laura Shenton 978-1-78952-070-5
Maximum Darkness – Deke Leonard 978-1-78952-048-4
The Twang Dynasty – Deke Leonard 978-1-78952-049-1

and many more to come!